Kevin Zraly's

AMERICAN

WINE GUIDE

Kevin Zraly's
AMERICAN
WINE GUIDE

Sterling Publishing Co., Inc.

NEW YORK

Dedication

To the pioneers of American wine making, the French, Italian, German, Spanish, Irish, Finnish, and all of the other immigrants who persevered first on the East Coast of the United States then to the Midwest and onward to the West Coast and now to all the 50 states.

To all the wine writers who critiqued the wines in the early days helping to improve the quality to where it is today—world-class American wines.

A special note on writers Leon Adams (*Wines of America*), Frank Schoonmaker (*Frank Schoonmaker's Encyclopedia of Wine*), Andy Dias Blue (*American Wines*).

Library of Congress Cataloging-in-Publication Data Available

10 9 8 7 6 5 4 3 2

Published by Sterling Publishing Co., Inc.
387 Park Avenue South, New York, NY 10016
© 2006 by Kevin Zraly
Distributed in Canada by Sterling Publishing
c/o Canadian Manda Group, 165 Dufferin Street
Toronto, Ontario, Canada M6K 3H6
Distributed in the United Kingdom by GMC
Distribution Services
Castle Place, 166 High Street, Lewes, East Sussex,
England BN7 1XU
Distributed in Australia by Capricorn Link
(Australia) Pty. Ltd.
P.O. Box 704, Windsor, NSW 2756, Australia

Sterling ISBN-13: 978-1-4027-2585-2
       ISBN-10: 1-4027-2585-X

For information about custom editions, special sales, premium and corporate purchases, please contact Sterling Special Sales Department at 800-805-5489 or specialsales@sterlingpub.com.

Acknowledgments

It was my honor and privilege to be able to work again with Inez Ribustello, former beverage director at Windows on the World restaurant in New York City, on her extensive research on American wines.

It is always a pleasure working with my editor and advisor, Steve Topping.

Thanks to Michelle Woodruff, the one who kept all the details together compiling the many labels, winery information, and editing between myself and Sterling Publishing; to Jim Tresize of the New York Wine & Grape Foundation; and to Bill Nelson of Wine America.

From Sterling Publishing: For the look of the book, Heidi North and Pip Tannenbaum, with designers Kevin Hanek and Laura Smyth; editorial contributions by Steve Magnuson, Rena Kornbluh, and Sara Cheney, with copyeditors Melanie Gold and Paula Reedy; cover design by Heidi North; shepherding the book in its early stages, Pam Horn; and project manager Rebecca Maines.

Contents

Introduction

AMERICANS ARE DRINKING American wine! More than 75 percent of wines consumed in the United States are from this country. The most encouraging trend over the past few years is that Americans are drinking wine on a daily basis, not only for its reported health benefits, but simply because it tastes good and pairs so well with all kinds of foods. While there are plenty of books written on French, Italian, and Spanish wines, there are very few available on American wines; and there is no wine guide that encompasses the wines from all fifty states.

This first edition of *Kevin Zraly's American Wine Guide* amasses the history, renaissance, facts, figures, and lore of American wine. It represents my first attempt to cover an industry and product that are making a discernable mark not only on these shores but also worldwide—and most definitely one that has sparked a passion within me. My own career in wine spans more than thirty years, and in that time two of the most notable—and, to me, exciting—trends in the world of wine have been the remarkable rise in the quality of wines produced in America and wine consumption in America. These two trends, of course, keep reinforcing each other, so we can continue to expect great things from American winemakers.

Another significant development for American producers and consumers came in a May 2005 Supreme Court decision that overturned laws in New York and Michigan that allowed residents to order directly from in-state wineries but not from out-of-state vintners. In a 5–4 decision in *Wine Wholesalers Association v. Heald,* the justices rejected the inconsistency of the New York and Michigan laws. For American wine, this could be the most notable ruling since Prohibition, and it goes right to the core of how the growth of American winemaking had previously been hindered. Outside of the "Big Four" states—California, New York, Washington, and Oregon—distribution has been the main obstacle to growth, especially for smaller wineries. With its ruling, the Supreme Court has thrown the matter back to the states to revamp their own laws to either allow interstate wine purchases or scrap mail-order wine sales altogether. Within months, New York had done just that, enacting legislation to allow out-of-state wineries to ship to the state's consumers while also permitting the state's two hundred-plus wineries to ship to consumers in all other states where such shipments are legal. I believe new wine distribution laws will greatly improve the availability of many wines from smaller, boutique wineries around the country.

American wine also has an enormous "fun factor." To me, studying and tasting the wines from around the country is truly exciting. It is a lesson in geography, history, agriculture, and the passion of grape growers and winemakers. But I am not just talking about wines from the four top wine-producing states. I get really thrilled finding undiscovered gems in Arizona, North Carolina, Idaho, and beyond. In fact, there are now wineries in each of the fifty states. When I began studying wine in 1970, two-thirds of the states had no wineries at all.

Visiting wineries in the United States has become a major tourist attraction. "Wine trails" have sprung up all across the United States in combination with other historical landmarks in those particular regions. Wine has definitely gone mainstream in America.

Searching for America

My own love affair with wine began in 1970 when, at the age of nineteen, I visited my first winery, Benmarl, in New York's Hudson Valley. That experience struck a nerve. I felt deeply connected to the earth, the grapes, the growers, and, of course, the wine. My soul was stirred; I knew after this first visit that I needed to learn more about wine, winemaking, and wine culture. I continued my early education by seeking out and visiting other wineries in New York State, beginning with wineries in the Hudson Valley and on to those in the Finger Lakes area. I made trip after trip, trekking from vineyard to vineyard.

But that wasn't enough. Each winery I visited provoked an urgent desire to see and learn more about wine. I had taken the first steps of what would become a lifelong journey. I began going to wine tastings as frequently as I could, sampling wines from all over the world. I studied grapes, learning each variety and its characteristics until I was able to identify most of the grapes used in the wines I tasted. And I became obsessive in my study of viticulture and wine tasting. The more I learned, the more I needed to know.

In the early 1970s the Finger Lakes district of New York and the North Coast of California were the only two regions in America producing quality wine. I will never forget reading, in 1972, the cover of *Time* magazine. The headline read *American Wine: There's Gold in Them Thar Grapes*, referring to the renaissance of California winemaking. So that summer (my twenty-first year) I took time off from college and hitchhiked west to California. I stayed for six months, visiting every major winery I'd heard of, tasting the wine and absorbing as much as I could about California wines and wine culture.

THE BEST-KNOWN WINERIES OF CALIFORNIA IN THE 1960s

Almaden
Beaulieu
Beringer
Concannon
Inglenook
Korbel
Krug
Martini
Paul Masson
Wente

On that trip I discovered that although some California winemakers were committed to producing fine wine, top quality American wine was still hard to come by. I found only a very few California wines worthy of comparison to the quality European wine I'd tasted. The best California wine was yet to come.

In 1974, after graduating from college, I traveled to Europe to tour the great vineyards of France, Spain, Italy, Germany, and Portugal. I was astounded by the extent to which each country possessed unique wine traditions, producing an impressive variety of superior quality wines. What struck me most was the difference between the Old World and the New. European wine was like classical music: complex, yet soft and memorable, nurtured and matured over centuries of tradition. American wine, on the other hand, was like rock and roll: young, brash, and new, honoring no rules.

Top 10 states in production of U.S. wines

California
Washington
New York
Oregon
Ohio
Virginia
Pennsylvania
Texas
Missouri
Illinois

A year after I returned from Europe, fortune smiled on me: I became the first cellar master at Windows on the World—the world-class restaurant atop the newly built World Trade Center in New York City. When we opened, our customers favored European wines, primarily French Bordeaux and Burgundy, which was fine with me. My time abroad had taught me how to taste, what to buy, and how long to age each. However, I was still drawn to American wine, so in the late 1970s, I arranged for a return visit to California. To my delight, this time I found, just as *Time* had predicted, that California winemakers were beginning to produce more and higher quality wines, some of which were comparable to the finest European offerings.

I came back to New York and immediately revised the wine list at Windows on the World. My original wine list had been 90 percent French. My new wine list favored American wine by a three-to-one margin. Our customers were cautious but adventurous enough to taste. Once they sampled and enjoyed the delicious Sonoma Chardonnays and Napa Valley Cabernet Sauvignons, they too became believers. By 1980, American consumers had begun to take California wine seriously. But California wasn't the only state producing good wine. Other states and regions, such as Oregon, Washington, and Long Island, were developing excellent vineyards and wineries as well. Word on the street quickly spread, and in culinary circles conversation often began with "Have you tried the Oregon Pinot Noir and Pinot Gris?" followed by "What about Washington State Cabernet Sauvignon and Long Island Merlot?"

Fast-forward twenty-five years to 2005. California still produces nine-tenths of all wine made in the United States, but New York, Oregon, and Washington State produce great wines as well. I can confidently say that for the first time in its history America is becoming well-known as a wine-producing nation.

Today I can enjoy a meal accompanied by wines from Virginia, Pennsylvania, Texas, or any of the fifty states. This couldn't have happened without Americans rediscovering wine over the last twenty years. In fact, we are now the third-largest wine-consuming nation in the world, with projections indicating that within the next five years the United States will be the top wine consumer worldwide!

Finally, our time has arrived. Thanks to the conviction and determination of American producers, the demands of American consumers, and the savvy of American wine writers, and in spite of the many obstacles that prevented more rapid progress, I can proudly say that many of the best wines in the world are produced in the United States.

CHAPTER 1

Wine Basics

BEFORE DELVING INTO the vast territory of American wines there is some basic information to learn and review about wines and winemaking. Your wine experience, whether in a retail shop or a restaurant, should be easy and fun—not frustrating. The information that follows will help you build and reinforce the foundation of your wine knowledge. This essential material has been culled from the most commonly asked questions in my Windows on the World Wine Course. These basics, along with an adventurous spirit, are the only prerequisites for an exciting exploration into the world of American wine.

Building Blocks

Wine is the fermented juice of grapes (and other fruits). Fermentation is the process by which the grape juice turns into wine. The simple formula for fermentation is:

Sugar + Yeast = Alcohol + Carbon Dioxide (CO_2)

Sugar is naturally present in the ripe grape. Yeast also occurs naturally, as the white bloom on the grape skin. However, this natural yeast is not always used in today's winemaking. In many cases, laboratory strains of pure yeast have been isolated, each strain contributing something unique to the style of the wine. The fermentation process begins when the grapes are crushed and ends when all of the sugar has been converted to alcohol or when the alcohol reaches about 15 percent, the level at which alcohol kills off the yeast. The carbon dioxide dissipates into the air, except in the case of Champagne and other sparkling wines, where this gas is retained through a special process.

Grape Varieties

The major wine grapes come from the species *Vitis vinifera*. Both European and American winemakers use *Vitis vinifera,* which includes many different varieties of grapes—both red and white. However, there are other grapes besides *vinifera* used for winemaking in the United States. Two of the best-known native grape varieties are the species *Vitis labrusca,* which is grown widely in New York and other Eastern and Midwestern states, and *Vitis riparia,* which is grown in several wine regions of the United States. Hybrids, which are crosses between *Vitis vinifera* and native American species, have also been planted in the United States, primarily along the East Coast.

Although there may be about a hundred different wine grape varieties planted around the world, for our purposes we need to concentrate on the few most successful wine grapes in the United States, which are all from the *vinifera* species. For white wines, Chardonnay, Sauvignon Blanc, and Riesling are the three major grape varieties. And for red wines, the major grape varieties include Cabernet Sauvignon, Merlot, Pinot Noir, Zinfandel, and Syrah. Concentrate on these grapes, and get to know the characteristics that allow wine drinkers to distinguish one from another as you begin your study of wine.

Grapes are agricultural products that require specific growing conditions. For example, most red grapes need a longer growing season than do white grapes, so red grapes are usually planted in warmer locations. Just as you wouldn't try to grow oranges in New York, you wouldn't try to grow grapes at the North Pole. The areas with a reputation for fine wines have the right soil for the variety of grape grown there and favorable weather conditions. Proper drainage is also a requisite. Weather considerations include the growing season, the number of days of sunlight, the angle of the sun, average temperature, and rainfall. The right amount of sun ripens the grapes properly to

give them the sugar/acid balance that makes the difference between fair, good, and great wines. Vines in the United States are planted during their dormant periods, usually the months of April or May. A vine doesn't usually produce grapes suitable for winemaking until the third year, but will then continue to produce good-quality grapes for forty years or more.

THE MOST IMPORTANT FACTORS IN WINEMAKING

Geographic location
Soil
Weather
Grape variety
Vinification: the actual winemaking process

Grapes are picked when they reach the proper sugar/acid ratio for the style of wine the vintner wants to produce. (Sugar concentration is measured as Brix.) Go to a vineyard in June and taste one of the small green grapes. Your mouth will pucker because the grape is so tart and acidic. Return to the same vineyard—even to that same vine—in September or October, and the grapes will taste sweet. All those months of sun have produced sugar (Brix) in the grape as a product of photosynthesis.

June
3% acid
0 Brix

July
2.3% acid
10 Brix

August
1.7% acid
15 Brix

Harvest
September
0.9% acid
22 Brix

The Brix scale is a measurement of percentage by weight of sugar at specified temperatures in a solution. It was developed in 1897 by Austrian scientist Adolf Brix.

Talk About the Weather

Weather can interfere with the quality of the harvest, as well as with its quantity. In the spring, as vines emerge from dormancy, a sudden frost may stop the flowering, thereby reducing the yields. Even a strong windstorm can affect the grapes adversely at this crucial time. Not enough rain, too much rain, or rain at the wrong time can also wreak havoc. Rain just before the harvest, like the record rainfall in the Northeast in October of 2005, will swell the grapes with water, diluting the juice and making thin, watery wines. Lack of rain, as in the drought period in California's North Coast counties in the late 1980s, affected the balance of the wines from those years.

A severe drop in temperature may affect the vines even outside the growing season. For example, in New York State the winter of 2003–04 was one of the coldest in fifty years. The result was a major decrease in production, with some vineyards losing more than 50 percent of their crop for the 2004 vintage.

A number of countermeasures are available to the grower. Some of these measures are used while the grapes are on the vine; others are part of the winemaking process.

PROBLEM	RESULTS IN	SOLUTION
Frost	Reduced yield	Various frost protection methods: wind machines, sprinkler systems, and flaming heaters
Not enough sun	Unripe grapes	Chaptalization (the addition of sugar to the must—fresh grape juice—during fermentation)
Too much rain	Thin, watery wines	Move vineyard to a drier climate
Mildew	Rot	Spray with copper sulfate
Drought	Scorched grapes	Irrigate or pray for rain
Too much acid	Sour, tart wines	Deacidify
Too much alcohol	Change in the balance of the components	Dealcoholize
Phylloxera	Dead vines	Graft vines onto resistant rootstock

Phylloxera

Phylloxera, a grape louse, is one of the grapevine's worst enemies, because it eventually kills the entire plant. An epidemic infestation in the late 1800s came close to destroying all the vineyards of Europe and the United States. However, the roots of native American vines are immune to phylloxera. After this was discovered, all the *Vitis vinifera* vines were pulled up and grafted onto phylloxera-resistant American rootstocks.

In the early 1980s, phylloxera again became a problem in the vineyards of California. Vineyard owners were forced to replant their vines at a cost of $15,000 to $25,000 per acre, costing the California wine industry more than a billion dollars.

Wine Characteristics

Color: The color of wine comes primarily from the grape skins. Removing the skins immediately after picking means that none of their color is imparted to the wine, and the wine will be white. Most of the quality sparkling wines of California are made with a larger percentage of red grapes than white, yet most of these wines are white. (The same is true of most French Champagne.) California's White Zinfandel is made from red Zinfandel grapes.

Tannin: Tannin is a natural substance that comes from the skins, stems, and pips of the grapes, and also from the wooden barrels in which certain wines are aged. It acts as a preservative; without it, certain wines wouldn't continue to improve in the bottle. In young wines, tannin can be very astringent and make the wine taste bitter. Generally, red wines have more tannin than do whites, because red grapes are usually left to ferment on their skins. Red wine grape skins also contain resveratrol, which is believed to help prevent some cancers.

Acidity: All wine has a certain amount of acidity. Generally, white wines are more acidic than reds (although winemakers always strive for a balance of fruit and acid). An overly acidic wine is also described as tart or sour. Acidity is a very important component in the aging of wines.

WHAT TO CONSIDER WHEN DETERMINING WHETHER A WINE CAN OR WILL AGE WELL

1. THE COLOR AND THE GRAPE:

Red wines, because of their tannin content, can generally age longer than whites. And certain red grapes, such as Cabernet Sauvignon, tend to have more tannin than, say, Pinot Noir, and age accordingly.

2. THE VINTAGE:

The better the weather conditions in a given year, the more likely the wines from that vintage will have a better balance of fruits, acids, and tannins, and therefore the potential to age longer.

3. WHERE THE WINE COMES FROM:

Certain vineyards have optimum conditions for growing grapes, including such factors as the right soil quality, favorable weather, good drainage, and the slope of the land. All of this contributes to producing a great wine that will need time to age.

4. HOW THE WINE WAS MADE (*VINIFICATION*):

The longer the wine remains in contact with its skins during fermentation (*maceration*), the more it will have of the natural preservative tannin, which will help it age longer. Fermenting and/or aging in oak also increases tannin.

5. WINE STORAGE CONDITIONS:

Even the best-made wines in the world will not age well if they are improperly stored. For long-term aging, the best storage conditions for wine are 55°F and 75 percent humidity.

Vintage and aging: The vintage indicates the year the grapes were harvested, so every year is a vintage year. A vintage chart reflects the weather conditions for various years: Better weather usually results in a better rating for the vintage. It's a common misconception that all wines improve with age. In fact, more than 90 percent of all the wines made in the world are meant to be consumed within one year, and less than 1 percent of the world's wines are meant to be aged for more than five years. Wines change with age. Some get better, but most do not.

Wine Regulation

Each major wine-producing country has government-sponsored control agencies as well as laws that regulate all aspects of wine production and set certain minimum standards that must be observed. In France, these regulatory responsibilities fall under the umbrella of Appellation d'Origine Contrôlée (AOC); in Italy it's Denominazione di Origine Controllata (DOC). In the United States, wine regulation is overseen by the Alcohol and Tobacco Tax and Trade Bureau.

Tasting Wine

You can read all the books written on wine to become more knowledgeable on the subject, but it is in the tasting of wines that you truly enhance your understanding. The following are the necessary steps for tasting wine. You may wish to follow them with a glass of wine in hand.

Wine tasting can be broken down into five basic steps: Color, Swirl, Smell, Taste, and Savor.

Color

The best way to get an idea of the color of the wine is to hold the glass of wine in front of a white background, such as a napkin or linen tablecloth. The range of colors that you may see depends, of course, on whether you're tasting a white or red wine. The table opposite gives some descriptions of the colors for both, beginning with the youngest wine and moving to an older wine.

Color tells you a lot about the wine. In the case of white wine, a darker (or richer) color may tell you the wine is older, because white wine gains color with age. Or it may indicate the wine was aged in wood, which also adds color. For red wine, a richer color may indicate a younger wine; red wines, when they age, tend to lose color. As a general rule, I say that if you can see through a red wine, it's ready to drink.

The color of both red and white wines is also influenced by the grape variety. For whites, Chardonnay usually gives a deeper color than does Sauvignon Blanc. For red wines, Cabernet Sauvignon is usually darker than, say, Pinot Noir.

When teaching about wine, I always begin by pouring a glass of wine and asking the class what color the wine is. It's not unusual to hear some describe the wine as pale yellow-green; others call it gold. Everyone begins with the same wine, but color perceptions vary. There are no right or wrong answers, because perception is subjective.

Swirl

Swirl wine in your glass to increase the flow of oxygen through the wine. Swirling releases the esters, ethers, and aldehydes that combine with oxygen to yield a wine's bouquet. In other words,

WHITE WINE	RED WINE
Pale yellow-green	Purple
Straw yellow	
Yellow-gold	Ruby
Gold	Red
Old gold	Brick red
Yellow-brown	Red-brown
Maderized	
Brown	Brown

swirling aerates the wine and releases more of the bouquet and aroma.

Smell

Smell is the most important step in the tasting process. (This whole activity should never have been called "wine tasting" in the first place— "wine smelling" would be much more accurate!) Humans perceive just four tastes—sweet, sour, bitter, and salty—but the average person can identify more than two thousand different scents, and wine has more than two hundred of its own.

THE HUMAN ELEMENT OF SMELL AND TASTE

Bouquet is the total smell of the wine.

Aroma is the smell of the grapes.

The "nose" of a wine is a word that wine tasters use to describe the bouquet and aroma of the wine.

The average person has five thousand taste buds.

Other sensations of wine include numbing, tingling, drying, cooling, warmth, and coating.

Once you've swirled the wine and released the bouquet, smell the wine at least three times. You will find that the third smell gives you more information than the first smell.

Pinpointing the nose of the wine helps you to identify certain characteristics that are difficult to describe. Many people ask me to tell them what a particular wine smells like. I prefer not to use pretentious words, so I may answer by saying the wine smells like an oak-aged Chardonnay. However, this rarely satisfies most people. They want to know more. I respond by asking them to describe what steak and onions smell like, and they say, "Like steak and onions." See what I mean?

The best way to learn your own preferences for styles of wine is to "memorize" the smell of the individual grape varieties. For white, begin by trying to memorize the three major grape varieties: Chardonnay, Sauvignon Blanc, and Riesling. Keep smelling them, and smelling them, and smelling them until you can tell the difference distinctly in a blind test. For the reds it's a little more difficult, but you should still begin with the three major grape varieties: Pinot Noir, Merlot, and Cabernet Sauvignon. Once you memorize their unique smells and can distinguish and describe them without using flowery words, you'll understand what I'm talking about.

I have developed a list of five hundred different words commonly used to describe wine, which is helpful to describe an individual wine's characteristics. Here is a small excerpt:

aftertaste	bitter
aroma	body
astringent	bouquet
austere	bright
baked/burnt	character
balanced	chocolate
big/full/heavy	corky

delicate	nutty
developed	off
earthy	pétillant
finish	rich
flat	seductive
fresh	short
grapey	soft
grassy	stalky
green	sulfury
hard	tart
hot	thin
legs	tired
light	vanilla
maderized	woody
mature	yeasty
metallic	young
nose	

Personally, I like my wine bright, rich, mature, developed, seductive, and with nice legs!

You're also more likely to recognize some of the defects of a wine through your sense of smell.

Following is a list of some of the negative smells in wine:

SMELL	WHY
Vinegar	Too much acetic acid in wine
Sherry*	Oxidation
Dank, wet, moldy cellar smell	Wine absorbed the taste of a defective cork (referred to as "corked wine")
Sulfur** (burnt matches)	Too much sulfur dioxide

*Authentic Sherry, from Spain, is intentionally made through controlled oxidation.

**Sulfur dioxide is used in many ways in winemaking. It kills bacteria in wine, prevents unwanted fermentation, and acts as a preservative. It sometimes causes a burning and itching sensation in your nose.

Taste and Sensations

To many people, tasting wine means taking a sip and swallowing immediately. Proper tasting, however, is done with your taste buds. You have taste buds all over your mouth—on both sides, underneath, and on the tip of the tongue, extending to the back of the throat. Don't bypass all of those important taste buds by swallowing too quickly. When tasting wine, leave it in your mouth for three to five seconds before you swallow. This warms the wine to your body temperature, and creates more smells, all of which will be sent to your olfactory bulb.

When tasting wine, be aware of the most important sensations of taste and your personal thresholds to those tastes. Pay attention to where these sensations occur on your tongue and in your mouth. As I mentioned earlier, we perceive just four tastes: sweet, sour, bitter, and salty (but there's no salt in wine, so we're down to three). Bitterness in wine usually indicates high alcohol content and high tannin content. Sweetness occurs when wines have some residual sugar after fermentation. Sourness (sometimes described as

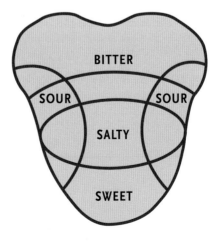

"tart") indicates the amount of acidity in wine.

Sweetness: The highest threshold for sensing sweetness is located on the tip of the tongue. If there's any sweetness in a wine whatsoever, you'll get it right away.

Acidity: Acidity is sensed at the sides of the tongue, the cheek area, and the back of the throat. White wines and some lighter-style red wines usually contain a higher degree of acidity than the more robust reds.

Bitterness: Bitterness is tasted on the back of the tongue.

Tannin: Tannin is not a taste but is a tactile sensation that begins in the middle of the tongue. As noted previously, tannin frequently exists in red wines or white wines aged in wood. When the wines are too young, tannin dries the palate too much. A lot of tannin in the wine can actually coat your entire mouth, blocking the fruit.

Fruit and varietal characteristics: These are not tastes, but smells. The fruitiness (the "body") will be felt in the middle of the tongue.

Aftertaste: Pay attention as the overall taste and balance of the components of the wine linger in your mouth. How long does the balance last? A long, pleasing aftertaste is usually a sign of a high-quality wine.

Savor

Once you've had a chance to taste the wine, sit back for a few moments and savor it. Think about what you just experienced, and ask yourself the following questions to help focus your impressions.

- Was the wine light-, medium-, or full-bodied?
- How was the acidity? Very little, just right, or too much?
- Is the tannin in the wine too strong or astringent?
- Does the tannin blend with the fruit or overpower it?
- What is the strongest component (sweetness, fruitiness, acidity, tannin)?
- How long did the balance of the components last (ten seconds, sixty seconds, longer)?
- Is the wine ready to drink? Or does it need more time to age? Or is it past its prime?
- What kind of food would you enjoy with the wine?
- To your taste, is the wine worth the price?
- This brings us to the most important point. The first thing you should consider after you've tasted a wine is whether or not you like it. Is it your style?

You can compare tasting wine to browsing in an art gallery. You wander from room to room looking at the paintings. Your first impression tells whether or not you like something. Once you decide you like a piece of art, you want to know more: Who was the artist? What is the history behind the work? How was it done? And so it is with wine. Usually, once *oenophiles* (wine aficionados) discover a wine that they like, they want to learn everything about it: the winemaker; the grapes; exactly where the vines were planted; the blend, if any; and the history behind the wine.

Most important, trust your own palate and do not let others dictate taste to you! The best definition of a good wine is one that you enjoy.

When is a wine ready to drink? This is one of the most frequently asked questions in my wine school. The answer is very simple: when all components of the wine are in balance with your particular taste.

The 60-Second Wine Expert

I ask students in my wine course to spend one minute in silence after they swallow the wine. We use a "sixty-second wine expert" tasting sheet for them to record their impressions. The minute is divided into four sections: 0 to 15 seconds, 15 to 30 seconds, 30 to 45 seconds, and the final 45 to 60 seconds. Try this with your next glass of wine.

Please note that the first taste of wine is a shock to your taste buds, due to its alcohol content and acidity: the higher the alcohol or acidity, the greater the shock. For the first wine in any tasting, it is best to take a sip and swirl the wine around in your mouth. Don't evaluate it. Wait another thirty seconds and take another sip, then begin the sixty-second wine expert evaluation.

0 to 15 seconds: If there is any residual sugar/sweetness in the wine, you will experience it now. If there is no sweetness in the wine, acidity is usually strongest in the first fifteen seconds. Look for the fruitiness of the wine and how it is balanced with the acidity or sweetness. What is the strongest component?

15 to 30 seconds: After sweetness or acidity, look for great fruit sensation. After all, that is what you're paying for! By the time you reach thirty seconds, you should experience a nice balance of all the components. By this time, you can identify the weight of the wine. Is it light-, medium-, or full-bodied? Start to think about what kind of food you can pair with this wine.

30 to 45 seconds: At this point you can begin to formulate an opinion of the wine, whether you like it or not. Not all wines need sixty seconds of thought. Lighter-style wines, such as Riesling and Pinot Grigio, will usually show their best at this point, and the fruitiness, acidity, and sweetness of a great Riesling should be in perfect harmony. For quality red and white wines, acidity—which is a very strong component (especially in the first thirty seconds)—should be in balance with the fruit of the wine.

45 to 60 seconds: Very often wine writers use the term "length" to describe how long the components, balance, and flavor continue in the mouth. Concentrate on the length of the wine in these last fifteen seconds. In big, full-bodied red wines such as the Syrahs, Merlots, and Cabernets and even some full-bodied Chardonnays, concentrate on the level of tannin in the wine. Just as the acidity and fruit balance are major concerns in the first thirty seconds, it is now the tannin and fruit balance you are looking for in the last thirty seconds. If the fruit, tannin, and acid are all in balance at sixty seconds, the wine is probably ready to drink. Does the tannin overpower the fruit? If it does at the sixty-second mark, I will then begin to question whether I should drink the wine now or put it away for more aging.

It is extremely important to me that if you want to learn the true taste of the wine, you take at least one minute to concentrate on all of its components. In my classes it is reassuring to see more than a hundred students silently taking one minute to analyze a wine. Some close their eyes, some bow their heads in deep thought, others write notes.

One final point: Sixty seconds to me is the minimum time to wait before making a decision about a wine. Many great wines continue to show balance well past 120 seconds. The best wine I ever tasted lasted more than three minutes—that's three minutes of perfect balance of all components!

How to taste wine

Step One: Look at the color of the wine.
Step Two: Smell the wine three times.
Step Three: Put the wine in your mouth and leave it there for three to five seconds.
Step Four: Swallow the wine.
Step Five: Wait and concentrate on the wine for sixty seconds before discussing it.

Chapter 2

American Wine: A History

Americans are now drinking more wine than ever before. In 2005, Americans consumed three gallons of wine per person, and sales topped $22 billion. A Gallup poll released in 2005 showed that, for the first time in the poll's sixty-year history, wine drinkers outnumbered beer drinkers in the United States. Fueled by an 18 percent increase in wine drinking by Americans, 39 percent of drinkers say they drink wine most often, compared with 36 percent who say they choose beer. How dramatic are these figures? Well, in 1992, U.S. drinkers preferred beer 47 percent to 27 percent. The growth in wine production has been similarly strong. In 1975, the United States supported 580 wineries, a number that has grown to nearly 4,000 today. For the first time in American history, all fifty states produce wine.

California is by far the leading wine-consuming state in the United States, with more than 42 million cases of wine sold each year. New York is a distant second, with 19 million cases sold. The next five states, ranked in order of wine consumption, are Florida, Texas, Illinois, New Jersey, and Pennsylvania.

U.S. wine consumers prefer American wines: more than 75 percent of all wines consumed by Americans are produced in the United States. Within the United States, California produces 90 percent of domestic wine, with Washington,

New York, and Oregon producing an additional 8 percent.

Before looking at specific American wines and wineries, it's important to know a bit about the history of winemaking in the United States. While we often think of the wine industry as "young" in America, its roots go back some four hundred years.

THE TOP FIVE WINE-PRODUCING COUNTRIES IN THE WORLD

RANK	COUNTRY
1	France
2	Italy
3	**United States**
4	Spain
5	Argentina

THE TOP FIVE WINE-CONSUMING COUNTRIES IN THE WORLD

RANK	COUNTRY
1	France
2	Italy
3	**United States**
4	Germany
5	Spain

THE WORLD'S TOP PER CAPITA WINE-CONSUMING COUNTRIES

RANK	COUNTRY	GALLONS/PERSON
1	Luxembourg	16.0
2	France	15.8
3	Italy	14.3
4	Portugal	13.0
5	Croatia	12.4
33	**United States**	3.0

Winemaking in the United States: The Early Years

The Pilgrims and early pioneers paved the way for American wine. Upon arriving in America, the early settlers, accustomed to drinking wine with meals, were delighted to find grapevines growing wild. These thrifty, self-reliant colonists thought they had found in this species (*Vitis labrusca*, primarily) a means of producing their own wine, which would end their dependence on the costly import of wine from Europe.

The early settlers cultivated the local grapevines, harvested the grapes, and made their first American wine. The taste of the new vintage was disappointing, however; wine made from New World grapes possessed an unfamiliar and entirely different flavor than wine made from European grapes. Undaunted, they ordered cuttings from Europe of the *Vitis vinifera* vine, which had for centuries produced the finest wines in the world. When the cuttings arrived by ship, the colonists, having paid scarce, hard-earned money for these new vines, planted and tended them with great care. They were eager to taste their first New World wine made from European *vinifera* grapes.

Vitis labrusca, the "slip-skinned" grape, is native to both the Northeast and the Midwest and produces a unique flavor. It is used in making grape juice—the bottled kind you'll find on supermarket shelves (think Welch's). Wine produced from *labrusca* grapes tastes, well, more "grapey" than European wines.

William Penn planted the first vineyard in Pennsylvania in 1683.

The three major types of wine produced in the United States are made from the following species of grapes:

AMERICAN:

Vitis labrusca, such as the Concord, Catawba, and Delaware grape; *Vitis rotundifolia* (commonly called Scuppernong); and *Vitis riparia*.

EUROPEAN:

Vitis vinifera, such as Riesling, Sauvignon Blanc, Chardonnay, Pinot Noir, Merlot, Cabernet Sauvignon, Zinfandel, and Syrah.

HYBRIDS:

A cross between two species, for example *vinifera* and *labrusca*, to produce such grapes as Seyval Blanc, Vidal Blanc, Baco Noir, and Chancellor.

Unfortunately, despite their careful cultivation, few of the European vines thrived. Many died, and those that did survive produced few grapes, which yielded very poor quality wine. Early settlers blamed the cold climate, but today we know that their European vines also lacked immunity to the New World's plant diseases and pests. If the colonists had had access to modern methods of pest and disease control, the *Vitis vinifera* grapes would have thrived then, just as they do today. However, for the next two hundred years every attempt at establishing varieties of *vinifera*—either intact or through crossbreeding with native vines—failed. Left with no choice, growers throughout the Northeast and Midwest returned to planting *Vitis labrusca,* North America's vine, and a small wine industry managed to survive.

Americans never really got used to the taste of this wine, however, and European wine remained the preferred—though high-priced—choice. The failures of these early attempts to establish a wine industry in the United States, along with the high cost of imported wines, resulted in decreasing demand for wine. Gradually, American tastes changed and wine served at mealtime was reserved for special occasions; beer and whiskey gradually supplanted wine's traditional place in American homes.

American Winemaking Goes West

Wine production in the West began with the Spanish. As Spanish settlers began pushing northward from Mexico, the Catholic Church followed, and a great era of mission building began.

The French Huguenots established colonies in Jacksonville, Florida, in 1562 and produced wine using the wild Scuppernong grape, a variety of the most common North American grape, *vitis rotundifolia*. Evidence indicates that there was a flourishing wine industry in 1609 at the site of the early Jamestown settlements. In 2004 an old wine cellar was discovered in Jamestown with an empty bottle dating back to the seventeenth century.

Early missions were more than just churches: they were entire communities conceived as self-sufficient fortifications protecting Spanish colonial interests throughout the Southwest and along the Pacific Coast. Besides growing their own food and making their own clothing, these early settlers also made their own wine, produced primarily for use in the Church, as sacramental wine was important in Church ritual. (Perhaps higher-quality wine was an important factor in attracting congregants!) The demand for wine led Padre Junípero Serra to bring *Vitis vinifera* vines—brought to Mexico by the Spaniards—from Mexico to California in 1769. These vines took root, thriving in California's moderate climate and forming the foundation of the first true California wine industry, albeit on a small scale. The early missionaries set up wineries in the southern parts of California, planting a grape variety known as the Mission Grape. Unfortunately, it did not have the potential to produce great wine. The first commercial winery was located in the area we know today as Los Angeles.

The Other Gold: The California Grapevine

Two events occurred in the mid-1800s that resulted in an explosive growth of quality wine production. The first was the 1849 California Gold Rush. With a huge surge of immigrants pushing steadily westward, California's population exploded. Along with their hopes of finding treasure, immigrants from Europe and the East Coast brought their winemaking traditions. Unsuccessful in finding gold nuggets, many discovered a different kind of gold: California's grapevines. They cultivated the *vinifera* vines planted by the early Spanish settlers and were soon producing good-quality commercial wine, although in small quantities.

The second critical event occurred in 1861, when the governor of California, understanding the importance of viticulture to the state's growing economy, commissioned Count Agoston Haraszthy to select and import classic *Vitis vinifera* cuttings—such as Riesling, Zinfandel, Cabernet Sauvignon, and Chardonnay—from Europe. The count traveled to Europe, returning with more than a hundred thousand carefully selected vines. Due to the climatic conditions in California, these grape varieties not only thrived, they produced good-quality wine. Serious California winemaking began in earnest. During this period the Civil War broke out in the United States, leaving the fledgling wine industry with very little government attention or support. Nevertheless, the quality of California wine improved dramatically over the next thirty years.

Booming Market Demand

In 1863, while California wines were flourishing, vineyards growing European grapes were in trouble. Phylloxera—an aphid pest native to the American East Coast that is very destructive to grape crops—began attacking European vineyards. While American native *Vitis labrusca* is resistant to phylloxera, Europe's *Vitis vinifera* is not. The infestation arrived in Europe on cuttings from native American vines exported for experimental purposes; it proved devastating. Over the next two decades, the phylloxera blight destroyed thousands of acres of European vines, severely diminishing European wine production just as demand was rapidly growing.

At this time California was virtually the only

region in the world producing wine made from European grapes, and demand for its wines skyrocketed. This helped develop, almost overnight, two huge markets for California wine. The first market clamored for good, inexpensive yet drinkable wine produced on a mass scale. The second market sought higher quality wines.

California growers responded quickly to both demands, and by 1876 California was producing more than 2.3 million gallons of wine per year, some of very high quality. California was, for the moment, the new center of global winemaking. Unfortunately, in that same year, phylloxera arrived in California and began attacking its vineyards. Once phylloxera arrived, it spread as rapidly as it had in Europe, leaving the same kind of devastation. The California wine industry faced financial ruin. To this day, the phylloxera blight remains the world's most destructive crop epidemic ever recorded.

Luckily, other states had continued producing wine made from *labrusca* vines, and American wine production didn't grind to a complete halt. By the late 1800s, California, New York, Ohio, and Missouri had become the major wine-producing states.

Shortly after the phylloxera blight reached California, years of research by European winemakers yielded a defense against the pernicious phylloxera aphid, by successfully grafting *Vitis vinifera* vines onto the rootstock of native American species

---

Honeymooning in the Napa Valley in 1880, Robert Louis Stevenson described the efforts of local vintners to match soil and climate with the best possible varietals. "One corner of land after another...this is a failure, that is better, this is best. So bit by bit, they grope about for their Clos de Vougeot and Lafite...and the wine is bottled poetry."

(which were immune to the phylloxera). These new hybrids combined the hardy disease-resistant rootstock of the native American *labrusca* with the variety and quality of Europe's *Vitis vinifera,* rescuing the European wine industry.

Americans followed, and the California wine industry not only recovered but flourished, producing better quality wines than ever before. In 1899 and 1900, American wines first won medals in international competitions, gaining the respect and admiration of the world. Forty different American wineries won medals at the 1900 Paris Exposition, including wines from California, New Jersey, New York, Ohio, and Virginia. And it only took three hundred years!

Prohibition: Yet Another Setback

In 1920, the Eighteenth Amendment to the United States Constitution was enacted, creating yet another serious setback to the American wine industry. The National Prohibition Act, also known as the Volstead Act, prohibited the manufacture, sale, transportation, importation, exportation, delivery, or possession of intoxicating liquors for beverage purposes, and nearly destroyed what had become a thriving national industry. In 1920 there were more than 700 wineries in California. By the end of Prohibition there were 160.

If Prohibition had lasted only four or five years, its impact on the wine industry might have been negligible. But it continued for thirteen years, during which time grapes went underground, becoming an important commodity in the criminal economy. One loophole in the Volstead Act allowed for the manufacture and sale of sacramental wines, medicinal wines for sale by pharmacists with a doctor's prescription, and medicinal wine tonics (fortified wines) sold without prescription. Perhaps more important, Prohibition allowed anyone to produce up to two hundred gallons of fruit juice or cider each year. The fruit juice, which was sometimes made into concentrate, was ideal for making wine. Some of this yield found its way to bootleggers throughout America who did just that. But not for long, because the government stepped in and banned the sale of grape juice, preventing illegal wine production. Vineyards stopped being planted, and the American wine industry ground to a halt.

Prohibition produced the Roaring Twenties and fostered more beer and distilled-spirit drinkers than wine drinkers, because the raw materials were easier to come by. But fortified wine, or medicinal wine tonic—containing about 20 percent alcohol, which made it more like a distilled spirit than regular wine—was still available and became America's number one wine. Thunderbird and Wild Irish Rose, to name two examples, are fortified wines. American wine was soon popular more for its effect than its taste; in fact, the word *wino* came into use during the Depression to describe those unfortunate souls who turned to fortified wine to forget their troubles.

Prohibition was repealed in 1933, but its impact would be felt for decades. During Prohibition, thousands of acres of valuable grapes around the country had been plowed under. Even after winemaking was decriminalized, wineries nationwide continued to shut down and the industry dwindled to a handful of survivors, mostly in California and New York, as Americans had lost interest in quality wine. Many growers on the East Coast returned to producing grape juice—the ideal use for the American *labrusca* grape.

The federal government, in repealing Prohibition, empowered states to legislate the sale and transportation of alcohol. Some states handed control to counties and, occasionally, municipalities—a tradition that continues today, varying from state to state and often from county to county.

ONE WAY TO GET AROUND PROHIBITION...

During Prohibition, people would buy grape concentrate from California and have it shipped to the East Coast. The top of the container was stamped in big, bold letters:

CAUTION:
DO NOT ADD SUGAR OR YEAST OR ELSE
FERMENTATION WILL TAKE PLACE!

Of course, we know the formula:
Sugar + Yeast = Alcohol + Carbon Dioxide (CO_2).
Do you want to guess how many people had the sugar and yeast ready the very moment the concentrate arrived?

Hard Times for Wine: 1933–68

Although Prohibition was devastating to the majority of American wine producers, some survived by making sacramental wines. Beringer, Beaulieu, and the Christian Brothers are three wineries that weathered this dry time. Since these wineries didn't have to interrupt production during Prohibition, they had a jump on those that had to begin again from scratch in 1933.

From 1933 to 1968, grape growers and winemakers had little more than personal incentive to produce quality wine. Many made inexpensive, nondescript, and mass-produced wines. These were commonly called jug wines, named for the containers in which they were bottled. The best-selling wineries during these years

were Almaden, Gallo, and Paul Masson. A few wineries, notably in California, were producing some good wines, but the majority of American wines in this period were ordinary.

SOME OF THE DILEMMAS FACING WINEMAKERS AFTER PROHIBITION

- Locate on the East Coast or the West Coast?
- Make sweet wine or dry wine?
- Make high alcohol wine or low alcohol wine?
- Make inexpensive bulk wine or premium wine?

The Reawakening of American Wine

It is difficult to pinpoint exactly when the American wine renaissance began, but let's start in 1968, when, for the first time since Prohibition, table wines—wines with alcohol content between 7 and 14 percent—outsold fortified wines. Although American wines were improving, consumers still believed the best wines were made in Europe, especially France.

In the mid-'60s and early '70s, a small group of dedicated winemakers, determined that California could produce wines equal to the finest of France, began concentrating on making high-quality wine. Their early wines, though not world class, demonstrated potential and began attracting the attention of astute wine writers and wine enthusiasts around the country.

As their product continued to improve, these winemakers began to realize that to market their wine successfully they needed a way to differentiate their quality wines from California's mass-produced wines—with generic names such as Burgundy, Chablis, or Chianti—and to ally their wines, at least in the minds of wine buyers and consumers, with European wines. Their brilliant strategy was to label their best wines by varietal.

Varietal designation calls the wine by the name of the predominant grape used to produce it: Chardonnay, Cabernet Sauvignon, Pinot Noir, etc. Savvy consumers learned quickly that a wine labeled Chardonnay would have the general characteristics of any wine made from that grape. This made wine buying easier for both wine buyers and sellers.

Varietal labeling spread rapidly throughout the industry and became so successful that, in the '80s, varietal designation became an American industry standard, forcing the federal government to revise its labeling regulations.

Today, varietal labeling is the norm for the highest quality American wines. It has been adopted by many other countries, and has helped bring worldwide attention to California wine. California's success inspired winemakers in other

Since 1995 the number of wineries in the United States has gone from 1,187 to nearly 4,000.

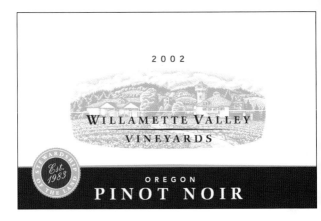

2002

WILLAMETTE VALLEY
VINEYARDS

OREGON
PINOT NOIR

regions of the United States to refocus on producing high-quality wine.

American Wine Appreciation

Buying American wine intelligently means having knowledge about and familiarity with each wine-producing state, as well as the regions within the state. Some states—or even regions within a state—may specialize in white wine, others in red, and, going further, there are even regions that specialize in wine made using a specific grape variety. Therefore, it is helpful to know

SIGNATURE

SERIES

2000
COLUMBIA WINERY
RED WILLOW VINEYARD
YAKIMA VALLEY
SYRAH

Celebrating 25 Vintages
1979–2003

A C A C I A®
2003
P I N O T N O I R
NAPA VALLEY - CARNEROS
ESTATE BOTTLED

ALC. 14.4% BY VOL.

the defined grape-growing areas within each state or region, called American Viticultural Areas (AVAs).

American Viticultural Areas

AVAs, specific grape-growing areas distinguishable by geographical features with delineated boundaries within a state or a region, are recognized by and registered with the federal government. AVA designation began in the 1980s and is styled after the European regional system. In France, Bordeaux and Burgundy are strictly enforced regional appellations (marked *Appellation d'Origine Contrôlée,* or AOC); in Italy, Tuscany and Piedmont are recognized as zones (marked *Denominazione di Origine Controllata,* or DOC). The Napa Valley, for example, is a defined viticultural area in the state of California. Yakima is an AVA located in Washington State; both Oregon's Willamette Valley and New York's Finger Lakes district are similarly identified.

There are about 150 viticultural areas in the United States (see map on page 49), 94 of which are located in California. The AVA concept is important to wine buying and will continue to be so as individual AVAs become known for certain grape varieties or wine styles. If an AVA is listed on the label, at least 85 percent of the grapes must come from that region.

Vintners are discovering, as their European counterparts did years ago, which grapes grow best in which particular soils and climatic conditions. For example, the Napa Valley, which is probably the best-known AVA in the United States, is renowned for its Cabernet Sauvignon. Within Napa, there is a smaller inner district called Carneros, which has a cooler climate. Since Chardonnay and Pinot Noir need a cooler growing season to mature properly, these grape varieties are especially suited to that AVA. In New York, the Finger Lakes region is noted for Riesling. And those of you who have seen the movie *Sideways* know that Santa Barbara is a great place for Pinot Noir.

Although not necessarily a guarantee of quality, an AVA designation identifies a specific area well-known and established for its wine. It is a

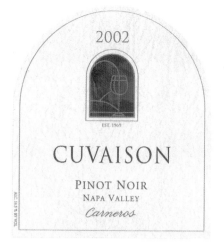

2002

EST. 1969

CUVAISON

PINOT NOIR
NAPA VALLEY
Carneros

point of reference for winemakers and consumers. A wine can be better understood by its
provenance, or where it came from. The more
knowledge you have about a wine's origin, by region and grape, the easier it is to buy even unknown brands with confidence.

Choosing American Wine

The essence of this book is to simplify American
wine for those who are buying (or selling) it. Do
you prefer lighter or heavier wines; red wine or
white; sweet wine or dry? To begin, you must
learn the general characteristics of the major red
and white grapes. Understanding these funda-
mental differences makes selecting an appropriate wine less difficult, as they help define the
wine's style—and selecting the style of wine you
want is the first decision you'll need to make.

Next, determine your price range. Are you
looking for a nice, everyday wine for under ten
dollars? Or are you in the market for a twenty-
five- or one-hundred-dollar wine? Set your limit
and stick to it. You'll find the style of wine you're
looking for at almost any price.

Finally, learn how to read the label (see page 170). Some of the highest quality wines in the United States come from individual vineyards. The general rule is: The more specific the label, the better the quality of wine. All the important information about any American wine appears on the label. Since the federal government controls wine labeling and has established standards, all American wine labels, regardless of where in the United States the wine was produced, contain essential information that conforms to national standards. This standardization can assist you in making informed decisions about the wine you're about to purchase or pour.

Proprietary Wines

The most recent worldwide trend is to ignore all existing standards by giving the highest quality wines a proprietary name. A proprietary name helps high-end wineries differentiate their best wines from other wines from the same AVA, from similar varietals, and even from their own other offerings. In the United States, many of these proprietary wines fall under the category called Meritage (see page 197). Some examples of American proprietary wines are Dominus, Opus One, and Rubicon.

Federal laws governing standards and labels are another reason select wineries are increasingly using proprietary names. Federal law mandates, for example, that if a label lists a varietal, at least 75 percent of the grapes used to make the wine must be of that varietal.

Imagine a talented, innovative winemaker in the Walla Walla region of Washington State. This winemaker is determined to produce an outstanding, full-bodied Bordeaux-style wine consisting of 60 percent Cabernet Sauvignon blended with several other grapes. Our ambitious winemaker has used his best soil for the vines, nurturing them with care and love. He has invested considerable time and labor to produce a really great wine: a wine suitable for aging that will be ready to drink in five years, but will be even better in ten.

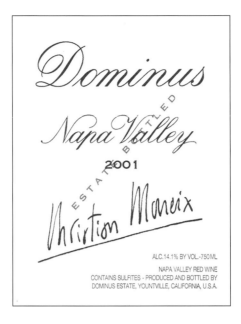

After five years, our winemaker tastes the fruits of his labor and voilà! It is delicious, with all the promise of a truly outstanding wine. But how does he distinguish this wine; how can he attract buyers willing to pay a premium price for an unknown wine? He can't label it Cabernet Sauvignon, because less than 75 percent of the grapes are of that type. For this reason, many producers of fine wine are beginning to use proprietary names. It's indicative of the healthy state of the American wine industry as well. More and more winemakers are turning out better and better wines, and the very best is yet to come!

This map shows the number of wineries and AVAs (see page 43) in each state at this writing. U.S. wine production continues to grow; new AVAs are registered every year.

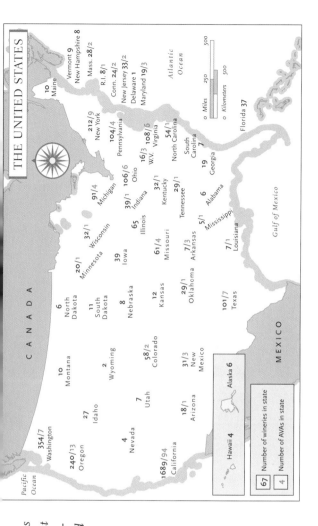

THE UNITED STATES

CANADA

MEXICO

Pacific Ocean

Atlantic Ocean

Gulf of Mexico

Washington 354/7
Oregon 240/13
Idaho 27
Nevada 4
California 1689/94
Utah 7
Arizona 18/1
New Mexico 31/3
Montana 10
Wyoming 2
Colorado 58/2
North Dakota 6
South Dakota 11
Nebraska 8
Kansas 12
Oklahoma 29/1
Texas 101/7
Minnesota 20/1
Wisconsin 32/1
Iowa 39
Missouri 61/4
Arkansas 7/3
Louisiana 7/1
Michigan 91/4
Illinois 65
Indiana 39/1
Ohio 106/6
Kentucky 32/1
Tennessee 29/1
Mississippi 5/1
Alabama 6
Georgia 19
Florida 37
New York 212/9
Pennsylvania 104/4
W.V. 16/3
Virginia 108/6
North Carolina 54/1
South Carolina 7
Maine 10
Vermont 9
New Hampshire 8
Mass. 28/2
R.I. 8/1
Conn. 24/2
New Jersey 33/2
Delaware 1
Maryland 19/3

Hawaii 4
Alaska 6

0 Miles 250 500
0 Kilometers 500

67 Number of wineries in state
4 Number of AVAs in state

Shopping in the U.S.A.

Today's wine buyer has thousands of choices. California has become one of the world's leading wine producers; Washington, Oregon, and New York State are producing more excellent wines in all price ranges; and now very fine wineries have developed in almost every region of the United States. But sometimes it can be very difficult to find some of these wines. Indeed, thanks in large part to the legacy of Prohibition, shopping for wine in the United States can be complicated and sometimes frustrating.

Perhaps I can help you find an easy path through this shopping maze by sharing some of the knowledge I've acquired over the last thirty years. I hope this section will be helpful for those who are interested in developing their own taste, building their own wine collection, or looking for a good bottle of wine for tonight's dinner. Let's begin by learning how the wine industry works, examining how it came to work this way, and exploring the primary ways consumers can purchase wine.

Most Americans buy wine either in retail wine and liquor stores or in restaurants. Buying wine in a retail store sounds simple enough: You walk in looking for wine. You're either shopping for a specific wine or looking for a new wine to try out with tonight's dinner. The point is, you want to buy wine and you're looking forward to enjoying it.

That simple shopping trip is often very frustrating, however. Buyers are often unable to find the year, label, or type of wine they're looking for. Instead they're confronted with an almost overwhelming choice of wines, many of which they know nothing about.

Why doesn't the wine shop have the exact bottle you want? Because wine retailing is different from most other retailing in the United States.

Wine Retailing

Small producers from the fifty states, not to mention all over the world, produce wine in limited quantities. Because their supply is limited, your ability to find exactly what you're looking for is chancy. The store you're shopping in might be sold out of the wine you want or might never have stocked the wine. In fact, it might never even have been offered the opportunity to purchase the wine in the first place.

Second, unlike food, clothing, or electronics, no national retail or distribution network exists for wines—and that's because of some uniquely American history.

Prohibition 1920–33

As discussed earlier, Prohibition taught the federal government that prohibiting the sale and consumption of alcoholic beverages created far more problems than it solved: U.S. citizens wanted their alcohol and they were going to have it. Crime rates rose and tax revenues fell. Still, upon repeal of Prohibition, the federal government took a very cautious approach to regulating the sale and distribution of all alcoholic beverages. Instead of setting up laws on a federal level, Congress decided to let individual states legislate intrastate and interstate distribution.

The result of this decision is that each of the fifty states has different rules and regulations, creating an enormous challenge for wine producers—foreign and domestic—in bringing their wines to market. In New York State, for example, an individual can buy a retail liquor license to operate a retail liquor store. That shop will be allowed to sell only wine and spirits, not beer. Supermarkets in New York are allowed to sell beer, but not wine or spirits. Across the river in New Jersey, there are many places you can buy food and wine in the same store. In Pennsylvania, wine and liquor stores are run by the state, not by individuals, and state authority sets pricing and selection policies. Some states make matters even worse by allowing individual counties and even municipalities within the state to set up their own rules. As you can imagine, this makes the distribution of wines and spirits in the United States an extremely complex business.

Wine Distribution

Given the complexity of a fifty-state system, the wine industry has set up a three-tier system of distribution. The system was designed to allow for areas of specialization along the cumbersome path of getting wine to consumers.

THE THREE TIERS ARE:

Tier I—Importer or winery
Tier II—Wholesaler (distributor)
Tier III—Retailer or restaurant

Tier I   Importers and wineries: The first tier comprises importers and wineries. A winery is self-explanatory: These are the winemakers who actually make the wines you buy in a wine shop or enjoy in a restaurant. The largest portion of all wine produced in the United States is sold by wineries directly to second-tier wholesalers.

Importers are buyers. They select wines from producers all over the world, sometimes entering into exclusive arrangements with them, negotiating prices, and shipping wines into the United States. There are also importers that represent some California wineries nationally.

Tier II   Wholesalers and/or distributors: The second tier of wine distribution belongs to wholesalers and/or distributors. One of their functions is dealing with all the rules and regulations of the state in which they reside. Some wholesaler/distributors operate in multiple states and have an intricate knowledge of the rules and regulations in many states. Wholesalers also play a key role in determining price. Negotiating with importers and wineries (remember, all wine is first brought to market through either importers or wineries), wholesalers negotiate how much they'll pay for each bottle they handle. They then sell directly to retail stores and restaurants.

Mergers and acquisitions have turned what used to be a small mom-and-pop wholesale business into a major corporate delivery system of wines to retailers and restaurants. For example, Southern Wines and Spirits, which began as a wholesaler in Florida, was, by 2005, operating in twelve states. The Charmer-Sunbelt Group, which began in New York, has wholesale operations in sixteen states.

It's not important for individual wine buyers to know the names of wholesalers. They're key players for the first and third tiers: wineries and importers, and retailers and restaurants. To the consumer, they're all but invisible.

Tier III   Retailers and restaurateurs: The retailer and the restaurateur are the best-known links in the wine distribution system in the United States, the links most familiar to wine consumers all across the country, and the links most important for you to understand.

Wine consumers have several different options when it comes to buying wine. The most common options are:

1   Retail stores

2   Restaurants

3   Wineries

4   Wine clubs

5   Wine auctions

6   The Internet

Because of the different laws of each of the fifty states, it's impossible to be specific about how you can buy wine in your particular state, county, or municipality. From this point on, I'll describe the ways most generally available to wine buyers throughout the country, and I'll give general advice about buying wine, which should be useful regardless of where you do your buying. But first, let's take a look at pricing.

Wine Prices

A winery will determine its prices by figuring out its overhead, production, and marketing costs, and then look to make some profit. Next, the winery sells its wine to the wholesaler. The wholesaler has to cover the cost he's paid the winery as well as warehousing, shipping, other expenses, and, of course, include his profit. He then sells to the retailer and restaurateur. The retailer or restaurateur buying the wine determines the final price that you, the consumer, will pay.

Retail pricing in wine is similar to other retail businesses. There are no fixed rules and no standard markups. But general policies do exist. Full markup equals 50 percent of what the retailer pays for the wine. In a competitive marketplace, some retailers sell wines at significantly lower markups. The average markup probably runs between 25 percent and 35 percent.

Retailers can use pricing as a marketing tool: Sometimes retailers sell popular wines at a lower markup—or even at cost, where permissible—as a lure to bring customers into the store, hoping that they'll buy other items at a higher markup as well. Some retailers discount prices as a matter of policy, appealing directly to the cost-conscious wine consumer. And since most wine is meant to be consumed within one year, retailers often put old or slow-selling stock on sale to clean out their inventory and make room for new wines.

The size and selection of the store, its location, and the knowledge of the owners and staff and the service they provide also determine pricing. If you are a serious wine buyer, find a good retailer in your area and develop a relationship with the staff. As a regular customer, you will get better pricing, good advice, and the most current information on wines you're likely to enjoy.

Remember, too, that wine is a precious commodity; good wines are not mass produced. Winemakers are essentially farmers, and their ability to produce top-quality wines depends on rain, weather, healthy crops, and good fortune.

THE THREE-TIER SYSTEM

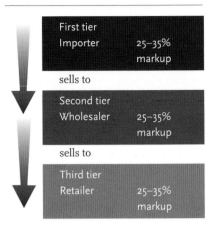

First tier
Importer — 25–35% markup

sells to

Second tier
Wholesaler — 25–35% markup

sells to

Third tier
Retailer — 25–35% markup

Wine Retail Store Options

Given that state laws vary, there are generally four types of outlets that sell wine at retail. They are:

1 Supermarkets and grocery stores
2 National retail chains
3 Other retail outlets
4 Wine and liquor stores

Supermarkets and Grocery Stores: A tremendous amount of wine is sold in supermarkets. Some wine publications even track total monthly wine sales in supermarkets broken down by varietals and style, to give an indication of overall national sales. The biggest advantage of buying wine in supermarkets is convenience: You can buy your wine at the same time and in the same place you're buying your groceries. Supermarkets often offer decent wines at reasonable prices. However, with some notable exceptions, supermarkets tend to offer a limited selection, often stocking only the most mass-produced and marketed varieties. These can be perfectly satisfying wines, but you'll have to do your own homework by buying and trying. Because wine is not their primary business, these stores seldom have knowledgeable staff and are unlikely to offer any special ordering service. But if your wine-buying retail choices are limited or you just prefer the convenience, try to shop in a supermarket whose selection shows some knowledge and imagination. Those are likely to be supermarkets with wine managers. Get to know the wine manager. Listen to his recommendations and if you find them satisfying, use him as a resource in trying new wines.

National Retail Chains: Where state laws permit, national retail chains have begun selling wine. Since their core business is focused on discount, it's possible to find some good wines at very good prices. Still, they are most likely to offer limited selections featuring the best-selling wines.

Other Retail Outlets: Drug stores, gas stations, and convenience stores are useful when there are no other alternatives. Prices can be attractive, but selections are likely to be very limited. If you're serious about wine, these are not retailers you'll be doing a lot of business with. Still, for wines under $20, they will probably have something worth buying.

Wine and Liquor Stores: Fortunately for the majority of wine consumers, there are retailers who specialize in wine. The staff members read the wine trade journals and are often familiar with vintages, producers, importers, vineyards, varietals, and blends from all over the world. They might sell wine exclusively, or they might be full-service wine, liquor, and beer stores. The heart and soul of the wine industry, wine stores are often owned and staffed by dedicated wine professionals. They take a keen interest in all the wines they carry, care about the tastes and demands of their customers, and will go out of their way to help you find a bottle of that special wine you had at a very expensive restaurant the night before. These are the shops you want to haunt. Get to know the staff, their tastes, and let them get to know you. The more they learn about your wine preferences, the more likely they are to recommend wines that will suit your tastes and to introduce you to wines you might not have otherwise tried.

An established relationship with a good wine retailer can also provide access to hard-to-find wines. Take California Cabernet Sauvignon as an example. There are more than sixteen hundred wineries in California and hundreds of them produce Cabernet Sauvignon. Some of the best and most sought after Cabernets are allocated by the producers to a few select retailers. Those retailers are given an allotment of wine—even they don't have an unlimited supply—which they offer only to their preferred customers. If you don't have a strong relationship with that retailer, you won't be able to buy the wine.

Choose a wine retailer with the same care and consideration you would use in choosing a great restaurant, an understanding therapist, a skilled doctor, an experienced lawyer, or a creative hairdresser.

Sampling Before Buying

This sounds like a great concept and follows my rule never to buy a case of wine until I've tried a bottle, but it can be problematic. While many grocers provide samples, the types of samples offered are limited, and what is offered is often

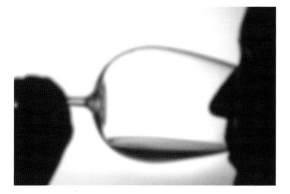

provided by the producer as a form of marketing. When were you allowed to taste a banana before buying a bunch?

Sampling exists in many wine shops in the form of wine tastings. Tastings are often supported by importers or wineries; they want you to try their wine, hoping you'll like it enough to buy a bottle—or more.

Quality wine retailers often host their own wine tastings, sometimes providing the wine themselves. There are also wine shops throughout the country that offer wine classes. Those retailers are committed to introducing their regular customers to new types and varieties of wine. They understand that everything in wine is about taste: If you like it, you'll buy it.

Of course, those pesky state regulations also play an important role in whether a store can offer wine samples. Remember, different states have different rules. Nineteen states prohibit any wine sampling in retail outlets, while fifteen other states impose a variety of restrictions. Some memorable restrictions are:

- Customers may receive only one three-ounce sample;

- A licensed salesperson may purchase one drink per customer;

- Only domestic farm wineries are allowed to be sampled;
- Never on Sundays!

Making Sense of Wine Ratings

Ratings are a fact of life in America, and it was inevitable that rating systems would come to the wine industry. If you understand how wine-rating systems work, you can use them to your advantage. Ratings began in the wine trade as a twenty-point scoring system to establish uniform standards at professional wine tastings. The twenty-point system assigns a numerical value to each of four qualities that professional wine tasters judge when they taste wine. As you look at how the points are allotted, you'll see what qualities professionals look for in a wine and how important each quality is in the overall rating. In the twenty-point system, each quality and its maximum value is:

Color and appearance	3
Smell (aroma and bouquet)	5
Taste (flavor)	9
Length and quality	3
	20 points

Consumer wine ratings began with a hundred-point system developed by the wine writer Robert M. Parker Jr. In the hundred-point system, every wine begins with fifty points. As the quality of the wine increases, so does the number of points it receives—all the way up to an orgasmic one hundred points! Nearly all wine publications and most wine critics have now adopted the hundred-point system. It's the system you're most likely to encounter in wine shops, catalogs, books, and magazines.

Opinions are divided on whether this is the best way to judge wine. Personally, I have no use for rating wine by numbers and believe you should judge wine by whether or not you like it. For consumers, a high rating gives credibility to a wine's quality. But be cautious in relying solely on ratings: If you consider eighty points a low rating, you might ignore well-made, reasonably priced wines with characteristics you would find appealing without breaking the bank.

You will encounter ratings as you shop for wine, whether in retail stores, on the Internet, in catalogs, or through wine clubs, so learn to use ratings to your best advantage. Study the critics with rating systems, choose the ones whose tastes most match your own, and buy accordingly. But keep in mind that critics are individuals too. As with movie critics, book reviewers, and restaurant reviewers, no one critic's opinion will ever exactly match your own.

Restaurants

The dramatic growth in wine consumption in the United States has affected the restaurant business dramatically. Wine lists are no longer the province of an elite group of high-ticket, white-tablecloth culinary temples. There are ever-increasing ranks of customers who actively seek to enjoy wine of all price levels in restaurants.

As a result, wine service has improved tremendously in American restaurants over the last thirty years. Diners are far more likely today to find intelligently crafted wine lists that complement the chef's food, along with waiters and waitresses who are better prepared to recommend

- Not enough wine lists for the number of tables
- Incorrect information, i.e., wrong vintage and producer
- High markups
- Untrained staff
- Lack of corkscrews
- Out-of-stock wines
- Improper glassware
- Overchilled whites and warm reds

wine and food pairings than ever before in the United States. Diners should expect at least this much from any restaurant they patronize. I advise everyone to apply the same care in choosing a restaurant—its food, service, and wine list—as I do in finding a good retail wine store.

One of the biggest challenges in dining out with a large group is choosing wine that matches a wide variety of main courses: meat, fish, and vegetarian selections.

I recommend ordering "safe" wines. My favorite choice for white wine is Chardonnay, either without oak or slightly oak aged. As for the reds,

my number one choice is definitely a Pinot Noir, especially from California or Oregon. These selections work well with meat, fish, and vegetarian choices.

Wine by the glass is the best thing that has happened to wine appreciation for both consumers and restaurateurs. Smith & Wollensky's restaurants sold more than one million individually ordered glasses of wine in 2005!

As a consumer, I only experiment with wine in a restaurant that has a good selection of wines by the glass or half bottle. This also eliminates the challenge of choosing a bottle of wine when one dinner guest orders fish and another orders meat. You won't get stuck trying to choose one bottle that will accommodate everyone's different menu choices.

Buying Direct from Wineries

Buying wine at wineries can be fun and exciting. A wine tour of the Napa Valley provides great scenery, good food, and a real education in how wine is made. You'll gain a better understanding of why each vineyard in a similar geographic area produces a unique product. You'll discover labels you may not know and find varietals that are often impossible to buy anywhere but at the source. You'll meet the growers and begin to understand the kind of passion, commitment, dedication, pride, and love they have for their grapes, their fields, their vocation, and their wine. Your knowledge of wine and appreciation of its complexity will expand exponentially. I encourage all wine enthusiasts to visit as many vineyards in as many regions and countries as possible. Visiting the source is a soulful experience. Plus, you get to actually taste the wine before you buy it!

But be mindful of how much you buy; the law in your state might limit you to what you can carry home. Shipping wine is subject to the same set of archaic rules and regulations that apply to the sale and transportation of all alcoholic beverages. Check your state, county, or local laws to find out whether you're legally allowed to have wine shipped to your home.

If you live in Southern California, you're in luck if you'd like to tour the North Coast wineries of Napa and Sonoma, taste some excellent wines, and decide to have them shipped to your home—intrastate shipping is perfectly legal. Many other states allow you to ship wine from California as well. But there are as many as twenty states where direct shipment from out of state is prohibited. There are states in which you would be committing a felony if you were to receive a shipment of wine at your home!

Many of these laws will be changing, thanks to a recent Supreme Court ruling. But it will take time for these changes to become effective, so, for the time being, check with the retailer or liquor control board before you make plans to ship any wine across state lines.

2005 Supreme Court Decision (*Granholm v. Heald*)

In May 2005 the Supreme Court, in a 5–4 ruling, struck down laws in New York and Michigan as discriminatory because they allow in-state wineries, but not out-of-state wineries, to ship directly to consumers. The cases were brought to the Supreme Court on appeal, with the plaintiffs claiming that the state laws discriminated against out-of-state wineries and therefore violated the U.S. Constitution's commerce clause, which prohibits states from intruding in interstate commerce. The states argued that they did in fact have powers to regulate alcoholic beverages, citing the Twenty-first Amendment to the U.S. Constitution, which, when enacted in 1933, repealed Prohibition.

The clear effect of the recent Supreme Court ruling is that as many as twenty-four states that currently bar out-of-state shipments will have to revise their laws so wineries are treated equally. This decision makes specific laws in six other states—Connecticut, Florida, Indiana, Massachusetts, Ohio, and Vermont—invalid, as are the reciprocity laws thirteen states had enacted to allow for direct shipping between them. These states include California, Colorado, Hawaii, Idaho, Illinois, Iowa, Minnesota, Missouri, New Mexico, Oregon, Washington, West Virginia, and Wisconsin. Again, the Court's ruling does not in itself effect any changes, but it requires the state legislatures to revisit their laws. The distribution from wineries throughout the United States will still depend on what each state legislature does. The impact of the ruling for now is that states must "level the playing field" and treat in-state and out-of-state wineries similarly.

In the case of New York State, a law was soon enacted to allow residents to buy directly from out-of-state wineries, whereas before they could only buy from New York producers.

Wine Clubs

Wine clubs exist to provide wine consumers with an easy way to purchase wine without leaving home. Wine clubs offer many types of service: Some automatically ship new wines to you each month; some offer special "club discounts"; some

offer proprietary brands; some offer rare wines; and some clubs offer wine novices an introduction to the entire world of wine by automatically selecting and shipping a selection of different wines—red, white, foreign, and domestic—each month. I did a quick Internet search for "wine clubs" and found more than three hundred listings.

My experience with wine clubs has been disappointing; I didn't find that they offered a better selection than a good wine retailer, and the rules and conditions of membership often aren't worth the trouble. But if you prefer the convenience of armchair shopping, look for a club that offers exactly what you're looking for, whether it's low price, automatic selection, or a wine education by mail.

The same interstate shipping rules apply to clubs that apply to all wine shipping. As you investigate club buying, first check to make sure the club can legally ship wine to you.

If you've thought about joining a wine club but your state doesn't allow delivery of out-of-state wines, there are other options. Check with your local wine retailer. Many have existing clubs and Web sites; those that don't will often set up a club just for you. Let your retailer know what you want: Describe your favorite wine color, regions, and price range, and decide how many bottles you want each month. Some retailers offer delivery to your door of wine especially selected for you and your taste.

Wine Futures

Think of the commodities market: Brokers race around the trading floor at the Board of Trade in Chicago buying and selling agricultural crops months, even years, before the crops are actually harvested. They're betting on future crop yields and market demand, both of which determine final prices once the crop is harvested. It's a form of gambling, with the broker hoping the price

paid today for a bushel of next summer's corn will be less than the price per bushel when the corn is harvested.

Wine futures are somewhat similar. When you buy wine futures, you are paying a retailer now for wine that hasn't matured and won't be ready to drink for some years (and in the case of extraordinary wines, will actually improve for decades). The retailer is in turn getting information about availability and quality from an importer. You'll be able to buy the wine at a lower opening price, and you're betting that the wine will age well enough to be of greater value than what you originally paid.

Wine futures started in France. As in the example of the commodities market above, it began as a way wine brokers could buy wine at lower prices before it was even bottled. It provided benefits for both the producers and the brokers: It gave producers immediate cash to help cover their operating costs and provided brokers greater opportunity to make more money. Brokers were gambling that the wine value would increase enough to recoup their original costs and yield tidy profits.

Investing in Wine

It wasn't long ago that outstanding California wines could find few buyers beyond serious wine collectors, who are always in pursuit of new wines, looking for wines that they believe are underappreciated and undervalued. These same collectors, after tasting the extraordinary Cabernet vintages of the early 1990s, realized the potential for these wines in the fine-wine market, and they bought all they could get. They brought the world's attention and focus to California wines,

introducing the larger market of individual consumers to California's outstanding product, while simultaneously increasing the value of their own California wine holdings. Now, because of the keen noses of those early collectors, the 2001 and 2002 vintages from the best producers of California Cabernet Sauvignon have already been sold. Nearly the entire production was bought by "new" wine collectors who are buying wines either to enjoy at a later date or to sell at a profit at auction in five years.

Investment in wine for profit is a relatively new phenomenon. Even the great Bordeaux châteaux didn't make a profit until twenty years ago, in 1982, when the illustrious wine critic Robert M. Parker Jr. declared the 1982 Bordeaux vintage one of the best Bordeaux ever produced. This created an enormous demand for the wine, which was quickly bought up by collectors and "investors." It was a great call on Parker's part, and the 1982 vintage Bordeaux did, indeed, live up to his description. It aged remarkably well and ten years later sold for nearly double its 1982 price. This has had a profound impact on the wine industry. What was once a quiet little hobby of wine collectors, connoisseurs, and savvy retailers has now become big business.

Market conditions today are different from what they were even five years ago for another reason: In the last ten years, there have only been four great investment-grade vintages in Bordeaux and four great vintages of California wine. Investment-grade wines aren't produced with predictable regularity. As with any speculative venture, investing in wine is risky: You need to be sure you're willing to take a loss if you decide to buy wine solely as an investment. Plus, you'll need to make sure you have the proper facilities in which to store your investment. And, of course, in many states it may still be illegal, at least until the repercussions of the Supreme Court ruling have settled, for individuals to sell wine without a license. You'll need to check your local laws before considering wine investments.

By all means, buy wine by the case and buy futures if you can afford them. Even if you don't make any money, you'll still have the wine, and while it may not have brought you great wealth, it will be there for you to open, pour, and enjoy.

CHAPTER 4

American Wine State by State

ALABAMA

STATE WEB SITE:
www.alabamawines.org

NUMBER OF WINERIES:
6

FIRST WINERY:
Perdido Vineyards, 1979

LARGEST WINERY:
Perdido Vineyards

WELL-KNOWN WINERIES:
Bryant Vineyards, Morgan Creek Vineyards, Perdido Vineyards

AMERICAN VITICULTURAL AREAS:
none

ACRES OF VINES:
650 +

TOP GRAPES:
Muscadine, Scuppernong

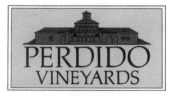

Alabama's First Farm Winery

Mardi Gras Red

A Sweet Table Wine

Alaska

State Web site:
www.americanwineries.org

Number of wineries:
6
Note: These "wineries" do not make wine out of grapes—they use wild berries, honey, and other agricultural products.

First winery:
Denali Winery, 1997

Largest winery:
Denali Winery

Well-known wineries:
Alaskan Wilderness Wines, Kodiak Island Winery

American viticultural areas:
none

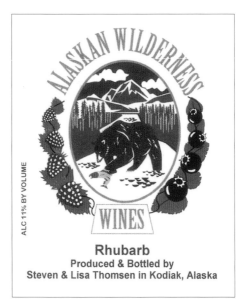

ALASKAN WILDERNESS

ALC 11% BY VOLUME

WINES

Rhubarb
Produced & Bottled by
Steven & Lisa Thomsen in Kodiak, Alaska

Sonoita

ARIZONA

STATE WEB SITE:
www.arizonawine.org

NUMBER OF WINERIES:
18

FIRST WINERY:
Sonoita Vineyards, 1983

LARGEST WINERY:
Kokopelli Winery

WELL-KNOWN WINERIES:
Callaghan Vineyards,
Dos Cabezas Wineworks,
Kokopelli Winery,
Sonoita Vineyards

**AMERICAN VITICULTURAL
AREA:**
1—Sonoita

ACRES OF VINES:
2,100 +

**U.S. RANK FOR ACRES OF
VINES:**
#9

TOP GRAPES:
Cabernet Sauvignon, Pinot Noir,
Viognier, Sauvignon Blanc

Arkansas

State Web site:
www.americanwineries.org

Number of wineries:
7

First winery:
Post Familie Vineyards, Wiederkehr Wine Cellars, both in 1880

Largest winery:
Wiederkehr Wine Cellars

Well-known wineries:
Post Familie Vineyards
Wiederkehr Wine Cellars

American viticultural areas:
3—Altus, Arkansas Mountain, Ozark Mountain

Acres of vines:
1,200 +

U.S. rank for acres of vines:
#13

Top grapes:
Cynthiana
Chardonnay
Zinfandel
Muscadine
Cabernet Sauvignon

PREMIUM WINEMAKERS

Post Familie

VINEYARDS

WHITE
MUSCADINE

SEMI-SWEET
ALCOHOL 12
BY VOLUME

Altus

CABERNET SAUVIGNON

Rare, dry red table wine with delightful color, bouquet and robust flavor of the famous Cabernet Sauvignon grape. Serve lightly at room temperature with almost any foods. Best with red meats or cheese.

Made and Bottled by Wiederkehr Wine Cellars, Inc. Altus, Arkansas. B.W.C. No.8 *Alcohol 12% by Volume.*

M-124 ATP

CALIFORNIA

STATE WEB SITE:
www.wineinstitute.org

NUMBER OF WINERIES:
1,689

U.S. RANK FOR NUMBER OF WINERIES:
#1

FIRST WINERY:
Buena Vista Winery, 1857

LARGEST WINERY:
Gallo

WELL-KNOWN WINERIES:
See Chapter 5

AMERICAN VITICULTURAL AREAS:
94

Alexander Valley	Benmore Valley
Anderson Valley	Bennett Valley
Arroyo Grande	California
Valley	Shenandoah Valley
Arroyo Seco	Capay Valley
Atlas Peak	Carmel Valley
Ben Lomond	Central Coast
Mountain	Chalk Hill

Chalone
Chiles Valley
Cienega Valley
Clarksburg
Clear Lake
Cole Ranch
Cucamonga Valley
Diablo Grande
Diamond Mountain
  District
Dry Creek Valley
Dunnigan Hills
Edna Valley
El Dorado
Fair Play
Fiddletown
Guenoc Valley
Hames Valley
High Valley
Howell Mountain
Knights Valley
Lime Kiln Valley
Livermore Valley
Lodi
Los Carneros
Madera
Malibu-Newton
  Canyon
McDowell Valley
Mendocino
Mendocino Ridge
Merritt Island
Monterey
Mount Harlan
Mount Veeder
Napa Valley
North Coast
North Yuba
Northern Sonoma
Oak Knoll District
Oakville
Pacheco Pass
Paicines
Paso Robles
Potter Valley

Red Hills Lake
  County
Redwood Valley
River Junction
Rockpile
Russian River Valley
Rutherford
Salado Creek
San Benito
San Bernabe
San Francisco Bay
San Lucas
San Pasqual Valley
San Ysidro District
Santa Clara Valley
Santa Cruz
  Mountains
Santa Lucia
  Highlands
Santa Maria Valley
Santa Rita Hills
Santa Ynez Valley
Seiad Valley
Sierra Foothills
Solano County
  Green Valley
Sonoma Coast
Sonoma County
  Green Valley
Sonoma Mountain
Sonoma Valley
South Coast
Spring Mountain
  District
St. Helena
Stags Leap District
Suisun Valley
Temecula Valley
Trinity Lakes
Wild Horse Valley
Willow Creek
York Mountain
Yorkville Highlands
Yountville

ACRES OF VINES:
800,000 +

U.S. RANK FOR ACRES OF VINES:
#1

TOP GRAPES:
Cabernet Sauvignon
Chardonnay
Merlot
Syrah
Sauvignon Blanc
Pinot Noir

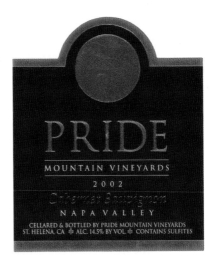

1996

ROBERT MONDAVI

NAPA VALLEY

FUMÉ BLANC

ALCOHOL 12.5% BY VOLUME

MASON

2003
NAPA VALLEY
SAUVIGNON BLANC

ALCOHOL 13% BY VOLUME

ARTESA

2002 CHARDONNAY

NAPA VALLEY

NEWTON

2002 CHARDONNAY

NAPA COUNTY 60% / SONOMA COUNTY 40%

PRODUCED AND BOTTLED BY NEWTON VINEYARD ST HELENA CALIFORNIA ALC 14.5% VOL PRODUCT OF USA ℮

PINOT NOIR   2002

Sea Smoke

BOTELLA

APPELLATION SANTA RITA HILLS

Santa Barbara County California

15.1% BY ALCOHOL

2003

PETER MICHAEL
— WINERY —

'L' APRÈS-MIDI'

SONOMA COUNTY SAUVIGNON BLANC ♦ ALCOHOL 14.2% BY VOLUME
ESTATE BOTTLED BY PETER MICHAEL
CALISTOGA, CA USA

RAVENS

WOOD

2 0 0 2

TELDESCHI

ZINFANDEL

DRY CREEK VALLEY

ALCOHOL 14.9% BY VOL.

B.R.COHN

2001 SONOMA VALLEY
CABERNET SAUVIGNON
Olive Hill Estate Vineyards

Contents 750 ml

Alcohol 14.0% by Vol.

RIDGE 2002
CALIFORNIA
MONTE BELLO®

MONTE BELLO VINEYARD: 74% CABERNET SAUVIGNON,
18% MERLOT, 8% PETIT VERDOT
SANTA CRUZ MOUNTAINS   ALCOHOL 13.3% BY VOLUME
GROWN, PRODUCED & BOTTLED BY RIDGE VINEYARDS
17100 MONTE BELLO ROAD, BOX 1810, CUPERTINO, CA 95015

MAYACAMAS

1999
NAPA VALLEY
CABERNET SAUVIGNON
PRODUCED AND BOTTLED BY
Mayacamas Vineyards
NAPA, CALIFORNIA, U.S.A. ALCOHOL 12½% BY VOLUME

FLORA SPRINGS

NAPA VALLEY

MERLOT
2002

14.2% ALC./VOL.

2002
Whitehall Lane
Leonardini Vineyard

Cabernet Sauvignon
Napa Valley

alcohol 14.2% by vol.

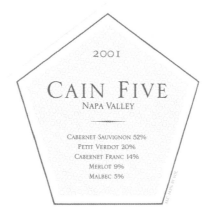

2001

CAIN FIVE
NAPA VALLEY

CABERNET SAUVIGNON 52%
PETIT VERDOT 20%
CABERNET FRANC 14%
MERLOT 9%
MALBEC 5%

MERRYVALE

2003

STARMONT
CHARDONNAY

NAPA VALLEY

ALC. 13.5 % BY VOL

RESERVE

1999

M

MARKHAM
VINEYARDS®

Merlot

NAPA VALLEY

ALC. BY VOL

IRON HORSE.
VINEYARDS

2003
ESTATE BOTTLED
Chardonnay

SONOMA COUNTY-GREEN VALLEY

ALC. 14.4% BY VOL.

GARY FARRELL
——— 2000 ———

DRY CREEK VALLEY

Cabernet Sauvignon

ALC. 13.8% BY VOL.

Bradford Mountain Vineyards

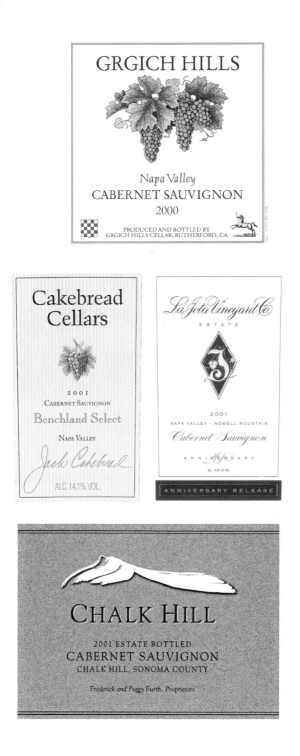

GRGICH HILLS

Napa Valley
CABERNET SAUVIGNON
2000

PRODUCED AND BOTTLED BY
GRGICH HILLS CELLAR, RUTHERFORD, CA

ALC. 13.9% BY VOL

Cakebread
Cellars

2001
CABERNET SAUVIGNON
Benchland Select
NAPA VALLEY

Jack Cakebread

ALC. 14.1% VOL

La Jota Vineyard Co

ESTATE

2001
NAPA VALLEY · HOWELL MOUNTAIN
Cabernet Sauvignon
ANNIVERSARY
ALC. 14.9% BY VOL

ANNIVERSARY RELEASE

CHALK HILL

2001 ESTATE BOTTLED
CABERNET SAUVIGNON
CHALK HILL, SONOMA COUNTY

Frederick and Peggy Furth, Proprietors

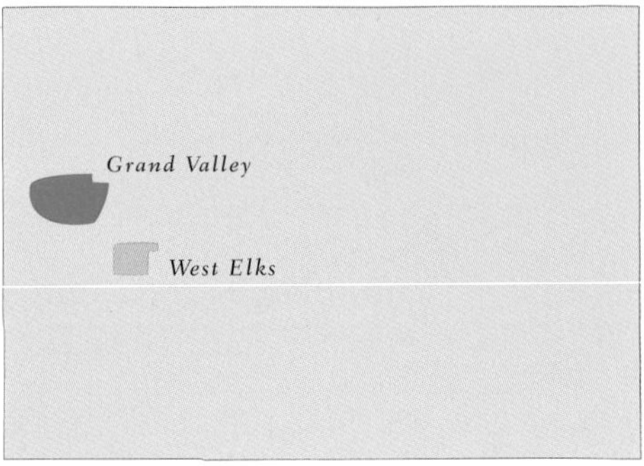

Grand Valley

West Elks

COLORADO

STATE WEB SITE:
www.coloradowine.com

NUMBER OF WINERIES:
58

U.S. RANK FOR NUMBER OF WINERIES:
#12

FIRST WINERY:
Ivancie Winery (now closed), 1968

LARGEST WINERY:
Colorado Cellars

WELL-KNOWN WINERIES:
Colorado Cellars
Garfield Estates Vineyard and Winery

AMERICAN VITICULTURAL AREAS:
2—Grand Valley, West Elks

ACRES OF VINES:
750 +

TOP GRAPES:
Merlot
Chardonnay
Syrah/Shiraz
Cabernet Sauvignon

COLORADO CELLARS®

Alpenglo™

2003

COLORADO
WHITE RIESLING

ALCOHOL 12% BY VOLUME

Rocky Mountain
Vineyards.

"Critter"

RoadKill Red™

2003

Semi-Sweet Colorado Red Table Wine
Alcohol 12% By Volume   Contains Sulfites

GARFIELD
E S T A T E S

Syrah

GRAND VALLEY COLORADO

2003

750 ML   ALC. 13.7% VOL.

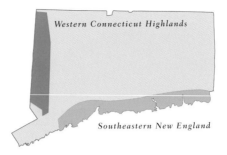

Western Connecticut Highlands

Southeastern New England

CONNECTICUT

STATE WEB SITE:
www.ctwine.com

NUMBER OF WINERIES:
24

FIRST WINERY:
Hopkins Vineyard, 1979

LARGEST WINERY:
Sharpe Hill Winery

WELL-KNOWN WINERIES:
Sharpe Hill Winery, Stonington Vineyards

AMERICAN VITICULTURAL AREAS:
2—Southeastern New England
Western Connecticut Highlands

ACRES OF VINES:
300 +

TOP GRAPES:
Chardonnay
Vidal Blanc
Seyval Blanc
Pinot Noir
Cabernet Franc
Cabernet Sauvignon

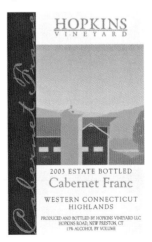

HOPKINS
VINEYARD

2003 ESTATE BOTTLED
Cabernet Franc

WESTERN CONNECTICUT
HIGHLANDS

PRODUCED AND BOTTLED BY HOPKINS VINEYARD LLC
HOPKINS ROAD, NEW PRESTON, CT
13% ALCOHOL BY VOLUME

Sharpe Hill

Select Late Harvest
1999
CONNECTICUT
VIGNOLES

ALC. 12%/ VOL 375 ML
PRODUCED & BOTTLED BY SHARPE HILL VINEYARD, POMFRET, CT

STONINGTON

Connecticut

CABERNET FRANC
2002

PRODUCED AND BOTTLED BY
STONINGTON VINEYARDS, INC. STONINGTON, CT 06378
ALC. 12% BY VOL.

HAIGHT
BLANC DE BLANCS
METHODE CHAMPENOISE
SPARKLING WINE

produced & bottled by Haight Vineyard
LITCHFIELD, CONNECTICUT
ALCOHOL 12.5% BY VOLUME

Delaware

STATE WEB SITE:
www.nassauvalley.com

NUMBER OF WINERIES:
1

FIRST (AND ONLY) WINERY:
Nassau Valley Vineyards, 1993

AMERICAN VITICULTURAL AREAS:
none

ACRES OF VINES:
10 +

TOP GRAPES:
Seyval Blanc, Cabernet Sauvignon, Merlot,
Chardonnay

FLORIDA

STATE WEB SITE:
www.fgga.org

NUMBER OF WINERIES:
37

FIRST WINERY:
Lakeridge Winery and Vineyards, 1989

LARGEST WINERY:
Lakeridge Winery and Vineyards

WELL-KNOWN WINERIES:
Lakeridge Winery and Vineyards, St. Augustine, San Sebastian

AMERICAN VITICULTURAL AREAS:
none

ACRES OF VINES:
1,100 +

U.S. RANK FOR ACRES OF VINES:
#14 (tie)

TOP GRAPE:
Muscadine

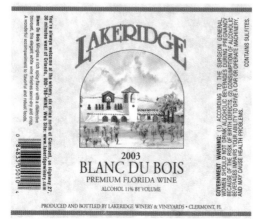

GEORGIA

STATE WEB SITE:
www.americanwineries.org

NUMBER OF WINERIES:
19

FIRST WINERY:
Georgia Winery, 1983

LARGEST WINERY:
Habersham Vineyards

WELL-KNOWN WINERIES:
Château Élan Winery
Frogtown Cellars
Habersham Vineyards
Three Sisters Vineyards
Tiger Mountain Vineyards

AMERICAN VITICULTURAL AREAS:
none

ACRES OF VINES:
1,600 +

**U.S. RANK FOR
ACRES OF VINES:**
#10

TOP GRAPES:
Muscadine
Cabernet Franc
Merlot
Cabernet
  Sauvignon
Chardonnay

HAWAII

STATE WEB SITE:
www.americanwineries.org

NUMBER OF WINERIES:
4

FIRST WINERY:
Tedeschi Vineyards, 1974

LARGEST WINERY:
Tedeschi Vineyards

AWARD-WINNING WINERY:
Tedeschi Vineyards

AMERICAN VITICULTURAL AREAS:
none

ACRES OF VINES:
30 +

TOP GRAPES:
Carnelian, Chenin Blanc

MAUI SPLASH
Passion Fruit
Pineapple Wine with natural fruit
flavors and caramel coloring

PRODUCED AND BOTTLED BY TEDESCHI VINEYARDS, LTD.
ULUPALAKUA, HAWAII · ALC.11.5% BY VOL · CONT. 750 ML

Idaho

State Web site:
www.idahowine.org

Number of wineries:
26

First winery:
Ste. Chapelle Winery, 1976

Largest winery:
Ste. Chapelle Winery

Well-known wineries:
Camas Prairie, Parma Ridge, Ste. Chapelle
Winery, Williamson

American viticultural areas:
none

Acres of vines:
1,225 +

U.S. rank for acres of vines:
#12

Top grapes:
Riesling, Cabernet Sauvignon, Merlot,
Chardonnay

Ste · CHAPELLE

2004
Johannisberg
Riesling
IDAHO
WINEMAKER'S SERIES

My kind of Wine!

VIN DE CITY RED

American Red Table Wine

ILLINOIS

STATE WEB SITE:
www.illinoiswine.com

NUMBER OF WINERIES:
65

U.S. RANK FOR NUMBER OF WINERIES:
#10

FIRST WINERY:
Lynfred Winery, 1979

LARGEST WINERY:
Lynfred Winery

WELL-KNOWN WINERIES:
Alto Vineyards, Galena Cellars,
Vahling Vineyards

AMERICAN VITICULTURAL AREAS:
none

ACRES OF VINES:
1,100

U.S. RANK FOR ACRES OF VINES:
#14 (tie)

TOP GRAPES:
Traminette, Foch, Chambourcin, Norton

Indiana

State Web site:
www.indianawines.org

Number of wineries:
39

U.S. rank for number of wineries:
#14 (tie)

First winery:
Oliver Winery,
1972

Largest winery:
Oliver Winery

Well-known wineries:
Chateau Thomas Winery, Dune Ridge Winery

American viticultural area:
1—Ohio River Valley

Acres of vines:
300 +

Top grapes:
Chardonel, Traminette, Chambourcin, Foch

Iowa

STATE WEB SITE:
www.iowawineandbeer.com

NUMBER OF WINERIES:
39

U.S. RANK FOR NUMBER OF WINERIES:
#14 (tie)

FIRST WINERY:
Ehrle Brothers Winery, 1934

LARGEST WINERY:
Summerset Winery

WELL-KNOWN WINERIES:
Eagle City Winery, Little Swan Lake Winery

AMERICAN VITICULTURAL AREAS:
none

ACRES OF VINES:
500 +

TOP GRAPES:
Niagara, Frontenac, St. Croix, Maréchal Foch

SUMMERSET
W I N E R Y

Caba Moch

Red Table Wine

PRODUCED AND BOTTLED BY SUMMERSET WINERY
1507 FAIRFAX, INDIANOLA, IOWA 50125

Kansas

State Web site:
www.americanwineries.org

Number of wineries:
11

First winery:
Smokey Hill Vineyards and Winery, 1991

Largest winery:
Wyldewood Cellars

Well-known wineries:
Dozier Vineyard and Winery,
Holy-Field Vineyard and Winery

American viticultural areas:
none

Acres of vines:
110 +

Top grapes:
Cabernet Franc, Syrah

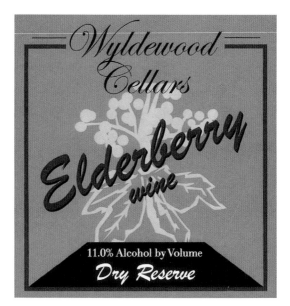

Ohio River Valley

KENTUCKY

STATE WEB SITE:
www.americanwineries.org

NUMBER OF WINERIES:
32

FIRST WINERY:
Lover's Leap Vineyard and Winery, 2000

LARGEST WINERY:
Lover's Leap Vineyard and Winery

WELL-KNOWN WINERIES:
Equus Run Vineyards
Springhill Winery and Plantation

AMERICAN VITICULTURAL AREA:
1—Ohio River Valley

ACRES OF VINES:
110 +

TOP GRAPES:
Cabernet Sauvignon, Merlot, Riesling,
Vidal Blanc

Mississippi Delta

Louisiana

STATE WEB SITE:
www.americanwineries.org

NUMBER OF WINERIES:
7

FIRST WINERY:
Casa De Sue Winery, 1992

LARGEST WINERY:
Feliciana Cellars

WELL-KNOWN WINERIES:
Amato's Winery, Casa De Sue Winery, Feliciana Cellars, Landry Vineyards

AMERICAN VITICULTURAL AREA:
1—Mississippi Delta

ACRES OF VINES:
30 +

TOP GRAPES:
Muscadine,
Niagara,
Blanc du Bois

Galvez
LOUISIANA SEMI-SWEET MUSCADINE TABLE WINE
GROWN, PRODUCED AND BOTTLED BY
FELICIANA CELLARS WINERY
& VINEYARDS, LTD.
JACKSON, LOUISIANA

MAINE

STATE WEB SITE:
www.americanwineries.org

NUMBER OF WINERIES:
10

FIRST WINERY:
Bartlett Maine Estate Winery, 1982

LARGEST WINERY:
Bartlett Maine Estate Winery

WELL-KNOWN WINERIES:
Winterport Winery, Cellar Door Winery

AMERICAN VITICULTURAL AREAS:
none

ACRES OF VINES:
40 +

TOP GRAPES:
Niagara
Chardonnay
Cabernet Sauvignon

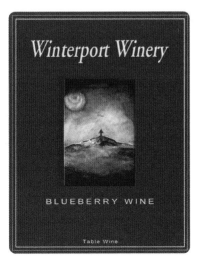

Cumberland Valley

Linganore

Catoctin

MARYLAND

STATE WEB SITE:
www.marylandwine.com

NUMBER OF WINERIES:
19

FIRST WINERY:
Boordy Vineyards, 1945

LARGEST WINERY:
Linganore

WELL-KNOWN WINERIES:
Boordy Vineyards, Fiore Winery

AMERICAN VITICULTURAL AREAS:
3—Catoctin, Cumberland Valley, Linganore

ACRES OF VINES:
350 +

TOP GRAPES:
Cabernet Sauvignon
Merlot
Chardonnay
Chambourcin
Seyval
Vidal Blanc

FIORE

MARYLAND

Cabernet Sauvignon

DRY RED WINE

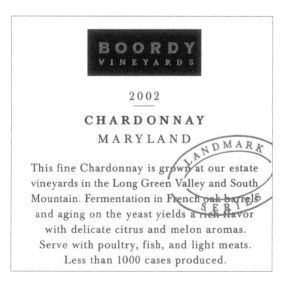

BOORDY
VINEYARDS

2002

CHARDONNAY

MARYLAND

This fine Chardonnay is grown at our estate
vineyards in the Long Green Valley and South
Mountain. Fermentation in French oak barrels
and aging on the yeast yields a rich flavor
with delicate citrus and melon aromas.
Serve with poultry, fish, and light meats.
Less than 1000 cases produced.

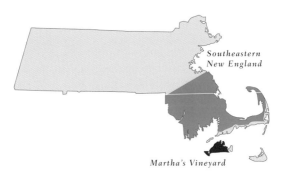

Southeastern New England

Martha's Vineyard

MASSACHUSETTS

STATE WEB SITE:
www.americanwineries.org

NUMBER OF WINERIES:
28

FIRST WINERY:
Chicāma Vineyards, 1971

LARGEST WINERY:
Westport Rivers Winery

WELL-KNOWN WINERIES:
Nashoba Valley Winery, Turtle Creek Winery

AMERICAN VITICULTURAL AREAS:
2—Martha's Vineyard,
Southeastern New England

ACRES OF VINES:
700 +

TOP GRAPES:
Riesling
Chardonnay
Pinot Noir
Voignier
Cabernet Sauvignon

BRUT

WESTPORT RIVERS

1998

CUVÉE RJR
Southeastern New England

TRADITIONAL METHOD SPARKLING WINE

GROWN, PRODUCED AND BOTTLED BY
WESTPORT RIVERS WINERY, WESTPORT, MASSACHUSETTS

ALCOHOL 12% BY VOLUME

CHICĀMA
VINEYARDS

Martha's Vineyard
Viognier

Vintage 2003   Estate Bottled

West Tisbury, Martha's Vineyard, Massachusetts
ALCOHOL 11.5% BY VOLUME

Leelanau Peninsula /
Old Mission Peninsula

Lake Michigan Shore / Fennville

MICHIGAN

STATE WEB SITE:
www.michiganwines.com

NUMBER OF WINERIES:
91

U.S. RANK FOR NUMBER OF WINERIES:
#9

FIRST WINERY:
St. Julien, 1921

LARGEST WINERY:
St. Julien

WELL-KNOWN WINERIES:
Château Grand Traverse
L. Mawby Vineyards
Peninsula Cellars
Tabor Hill
Winery at Black Star Farms

AMERICAN VITICULTURAL AREAS:
4— Fennville, Lake Michigan Shore, Leelanau
Peninsula, Old Mission Peninsula

ACRES OF VINES:
1,500 +

U.S. RANK FOR ACRES OF VINES:
#11

TOP GRAPES:
Pinot Noir, Chardonnay, Riesling,
Gewürztraminer, Chancellor

SHADY LANE

2002
PINOT NOIR
LEELANAU PENINSULA
ALC. 12% BY VOL./ 750ML

CHÂTEAU
GRAND
TRAVERSE
LATE HARVEST
JOHANNISBERG RIESLING
2004
ALCOHOL 10.5% BY VOLUME

GRAND MARK
Methode Champenoise
LAKE MICHIGAN SHORE APPELLATION

PRODUCED AND BOTTLED BY TABOR HILL WINERY   BUCHANAN, BERRIEN COUNTY, MICHIGAN 49107   BW-MI-37
SPARKLING WINE   ALCOHOL 12 1/2% BY VOLUME   750 ML
CONTAINS SULFITES

SEX
SPARKLING   WINE
BRUT   2125 OF 2574 BOTTLES
ROSE   BATCH #8
ALCOHOL 12% BY VOLUME   750 ML

L. MAWBY

Blanc de Blanc
BRUT   LEELANAU PENINSULA   ALCOHOL 12% VOLUME
0890 OF 3290   SPARKLING WINE
         BOTTLES METHODE CHAMPENOISE   750 ML

MINNESOTA

STATE WEB SITE:
www.mngrapes.com

NUMBER OF WINERIES:
20

FIRST WINERY:
Alexis Bailly Vineyard, 1978

LARGEST WINERY:
Carlos Creek Winery

WELL-KNOWN WINERIES:
Alexis Bailly Vineyard, Northern Vineyards

AMERICAN VITICULTURAL AREA:
1—Alexandria Lakes

ACRES OF VINES:
150 +

TOP GRAPES:
Frontenac, Foch, St. Croix, Prairie Star

MISSISSIPPI

STATE WEB SITE:
www.american
wineries.org

**NUMBER OF
WINERIES:**
5

FIRST WINERY:
Old South Winery, 1979

**AMERICAN
VITICULTURAL
AREA:**
1—Mississippi Delta

ACRES OF VINES:
400 +

TOP GRAPE:
Muscadine

Mississippi Delta

Old South

Miss Scarlett
Sweet Muscadine Table Wine
Mississippi Native Wine

MISSOURI

STATE WEB SITE:
www.missouriwine.org

NUMBER OF WINERIES:
61

U.S. RANK FOR NUMBER OF WINERIES:
#11

FIRST WINERY:
Stone Hill Winery, 1847

LARGEST WINERY:
Stone Hill Winery

WELL-KNOWN WINERIES:
Les Bourgeois Winery and Vineyards,
Montelle Winery, Stone Hill Winery

AMERICAN VITICULTURAL AREAS:
4—Augusta, Hermann, Ozark Highlands,
Ozark Mountain

ACRES OF VINES:
1,100 +

U.S. RANK FOR ACRES OF VINES:
#14 (tie)

TOP GRAPES:
Cynthiana
Vignoles
Seyval Blanc
Norton
Chambourcin

Montana

State Web site:
www.americanwineries.org

Number of wineries:
10

First winery:
Lolo Peak Winery, 1998

Largest winery:
Lolo Peak Winery

Well-known wineries:
Lolo Peak Winery,
Rattlesnake Creek
Vineyard

American viticultural areas:
none

Acres of vines:
20 +

Top grapes:
Maréchal Foch
Frontenac
Leon Millot
St. Croix

Nebraska

State Web site:
www.nebraskawines.com

Number of wineries:
8

First winery:
Cuthills Vineyards, 1994

Largest winery:
James Arthur Vineyards

Well-known wineries:
Cuthills Vineyards, James Arthur Vineyards

American viticultural areas:
none

Acres of vines:
300 +

Top grapes:
Edelweiss, St. Croix, Maréchal Foch,
Seyval Blanc

Nevada

STATE WEB SITE:
www.americanwineries.org

NUMBER OF WINERIES:
4

FIRST WINERY:
Pahrump Valley Winery, 1990

LARGEST WINERY:
Pahrump Valley Winery

WELL-KNOWN WINERIES:
Pahrump Valley Winery,
Tahoe Ridge Vineyards

AMERICAN VITICULTURAL AREAS:
none

ACRES OF VINES:
10 +

TOP GRAPES:
Cabernet Sauvignon, Merlot, Chardonnay

Pahrump
Valley Winery

American
SYMPHONY

VINTED AND BOTTLED BY PAHRUMP VALLEY WINERY
PAHRUMP, NEVADA 89048 BONDED WINERY BW NV 5.
ALCOHOL 12% BY VOLUME. 750ML. **CONTAINS SULFITES.**

New Hampshire

State Web site:
www.americanwineries.org

Number of wineries:
8

First winery:
Jewell Towne Vineyards, 1990

Largest winery:
Jewell Towne Vineyards

Well-known wineries:
Flag Hill Winery, Jewell Towne Vineyards

American viticultural areas:
none

Acres of vines:
20 +

Top grapes:
Maréchal Foch, Seyval Blanc, Vignoles, Chardonnay

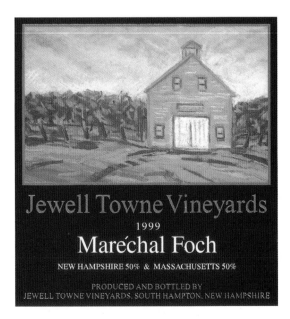

Jewell Towne Vineyards
1999
Maréchal Foch
NEW HAMPSHIRE 50% & MASSACHUSETTS 50%
PRODUCED AND BOTTLED BY
JEWELL TOWNE VINEYARDS, SOUTH HAMPTON, NEW HAMPSHIRE

NEW JERSEY

STATE WEB SITE:
www.newjerseywines.com

NUMBER OF WINERIES:
33

FIRST WINERY:
Renault Winery, 1864

LARGEST WINERY:
Tomasello

WELL-KNOWN WINERIES:
Renault Winery,
Tomasello Winery

AMERICAN VITICULTURAL AREAS:
2—Central Delaware Valley, Warren Hills

ACRES OF VINES:
1,000 +

TOP GRAPES:
Riesling
Chambourcin
Cabernet Franc
Vidal Blanc
Seyval Blanc
Pinot Noir
Chardonnay

2 0 0 3
Atlantic County, New Jersey
CHAMBOURCIN
Tomasello Winery
PRODUCED & BOTTLED BY TOMASELLO WINERY, HAMMONTON, NJ USA
ALC. 12.5% BY VOL.

NEW MEXICO

STATE WEB SITE:
www.nmwine.net

NUMBER OF WINERIES:
31

FIRST WINERY:
La Vina Winery, 1977

LARGEST WINERY:
St. Clair Winery

WELL-KNOWN WINERIES:
Casa Rondeña, Gruet Winery, San Felipe Winery

AMERICAN VITICULTURAL AREAS:
3—Mesilla Valley, Middle Rio Grande Valley,
Mimbres Valley

ACRES OF VINES:
500 +

TOP GRAPES:
Cabernet Sauvignon
Chardonnay
Johannisberg Riesling
Merlot
Pinot Noir
Sauvignon Blanc
Zinfandel

14.3% Alcohol by Vol.   375 ML
2004
Dessert Wine
Gewürztraminer
New Mexico
Estate   Bottled
Casa Rondeña
Winery
Los Ranchos Vineyard
Vinted & Bottled
by John R. Calvin

BlueTeal
VINEYARDS
2002
New Mexico
White Merlot
PRODUCED & BOTTLED BY
NEW MEXICO WINERIES, INC., DEMING, NM
ALCOHOL 12% BY VOLUME

ST. CLAIR
W I N E R Y
2003
NEW MEXICO
Reserve
MERLOT
ALC 13% BY VOL

NEW YORK

STATE WEB SITE:
www.newyorkwines.org

NUMBER OF WINERIES:
212

U.S. RANK FOR NUMBER OF WINERIES:
#4

FIRST WINERY:
Brotherhood Winery, 1839

LARGEST WINERY:
Canandaigua Wine Company

WELL-KNOWN WINERIES:
See Chapter 5

AMERICAN VITICULTURAL AREAS:
9—Cayuga Lake
Finger Lakes
The Hamptons
Hudson River Region
Lake Erie
Long Island
Niagara Escarpment
North Fork of Long Island
Seneca Lake

ACRES OF VINES:
31,000 +

U.S. RANK FOR ACRES OF VINES:
#2

TOP GRAPES:
Merlot
Cabernet Franc
Riesling
Chardonnay
Cabernet Sauvignon
Pinot Noir

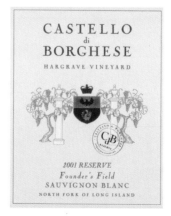

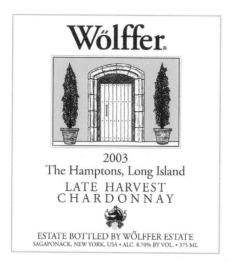

Wölffer

2003
The Hamptons, Long Island
LATE HARVEST
CHARDONNAY

ESTATE BOTTLED BY WÖLFFER ESTATE
SAGAPONACK, NEW YORK, USA • ALC. 8.70% BY VOL. • 375 ML

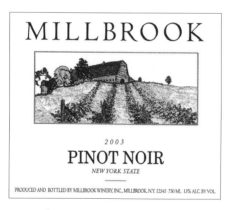

MILLBROOK

2003

PINOT NOIR

NEW YORK STATE

PRODUCED AND BOTTLED BY MILLBROOK WINERY, INC., MILLBROOK, N.Y. 12545 750 ML 13% ALC. BY VOL.

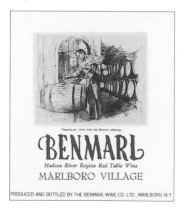

"Topping-up", Print from the Benmarl collection.

BENMARL

Hudson River Region Red Table Wine

MARLBORO VILLAGE

PRODUCED AND BOTTLED BY THE BENMARL WINE CO. LTD., MARLBORO, N.Y.

Yadkin Valley

North Carolina

State Web site:
www.ncwine.org

Number of wineries:
54

U.S. rank for number of wineries:
#13

First winery:
Medoc Vineyards, 1835

Largest winery:
Biltmore Estate

Well-known wineries:
Biltmore Estate Winery, RagApple Lassie Vineyards, RayLen Vineyards, Shelton Vineyards

American viticultural area:
1—Yadkin Valley

Acres of vines:
950 +

Top grapes:
Scuppernong
Chardonnay
Cabernet Sauvignon
Merlot
Viognier
Cabernet Franc

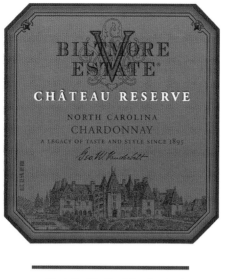

BILTMORE
ESTATE®
CHÂTEAU RESERVE

NORTH CAROLINA
CHARDONNAY
A LEGACY OF TASTE AND STYLE SINCE 1895

SHELTON®
VINEYARDS

ESTATE
BOTTLED

YADKIN VALLEY
Cabernet Sauvignon
2002
12.8% ALCOHOL BY VOLUME

BILTMORE
ESTATE®

AMERICAN
CABERNET SAUVIGNON
A LEGACY OF TASTE AND STYLE
SINCE 1895

North Dakota

State Web site:
www.americanwineries.org

Number of wineries:
6

First winery:
Pointe of View Winery, 2002

Largest winery:
Pointe of View Winery

Well-known wineries:
Maple River Winery, Point of View Winery

American viticultural areas:
none

Acres of vines:
3 +

Top grapes:
Frontenac, Prairie Star

Maple River Winery

Apple Jalapeno Pepper Wine

ALC 10% by vol.   750 ml

OHIO

STATE WEB SITE:
www.ohiowines.org

NUMBER OF WINERIES:
106

U.S. RANK FOR NUMBER OF WINERIES:
#6

FIRST WINERY:
Meiers Winery, 1856

LARGEST WINERY:
Meiers Winery

WELL-KNOWN WINERIES:
Ferrante Winery, Klingshirn Winery, Harpersfield Winery

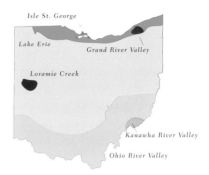

Isle St. George

Lake Erie

Grand River Valley

Loramie Creek

Kanawha River Valley

Ohio River Valley

AMERICAN VITICULTURAL AREAS:
6—Grand River Valley
Isle St. George
Kanawha River Valley
Lake Erie
Loramie Creek
Ohio River Valley

ACRES OF VINES:
2,200 +

U.S. RANK FOR ACRES OF VINES:
#8

TOP GRAPES:
Riesling
Chardonnay
Pinot Gris
Cabernet Franc
Cabernet Sauvignon
Pinot Noir

MEIER'S 44
AMERICAN
CREAM SHERRY
ALCOHOL 18% BY VOLUME

Ozark Mountain

OKLAHOMA

STATE WEB SITE:
www.oklahomawines.org

NUMBER OF WINERIES:
29

FIRST WINERY:
Cimarron Cellars, 1983

LARGEST WINERY:
Tidal School Vineyards

WELL-KNOWN WINERIES:
Stone Bluff Cellars, Tidal School Vineyards

AMERICAN VITICULTURAL AREA:
1—Ozark Mountain

ACRES OF VINES:
300 +

TOP GRAPES:
Cynthiana
Vignoles
Chardonnay
Shiraz
Zinfandel
Riesling

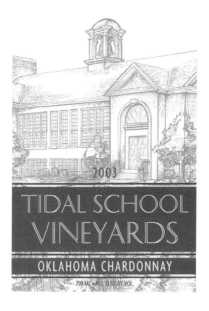

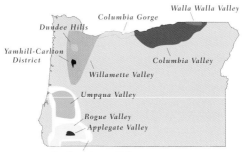

Oregon

State Web site:
www.oregonwine.org

Number of wineries:
240

U.S. rank for number of wineries:
#3

First winery:
Hillcrest Vineyards, 1961

Largest winery:
Willamette Valley Vineyards

Well-known wineries:
See Chapter 5

American viticultural areas:
13—Applegate Valley
Columbia Gorge
Columbia Valley
Dundee Hills
McMinnville
Red Hill Douglas County
Ribbon Ridge
Rogue Valley
Southern Oregon
Umpqua Valley
Walla Walla Valley
Willamette Valley
Yamhill-Carlton District

ACRES OF VINES:
11,300 +

U.S. RANK FOR ACRES OF VINES:
#5

TOP GRAPES:
Chardonnay, Pinot Gris, Pinot Noir

BENTON·LANE

OREGON
20 PINOT NOIR 03

Alc. 13.6% by vol.

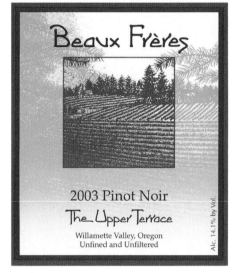

Beaux Frères

2003 Pinot Noir
The Upper Terrace

Willamette Valley, Oregon
Unfined and Unfiltered

Alc. 14.1% by Vol.

Rosé d'Or

Brut Rosé
Oregon Sparkling Wine
R·STUART&Co.

Bryce **viognier**

2003
Viognier
WillametteValley
DEUX VERT VINEYARD

ALC. 14.5% BY VOL.

■ 2 0 0 3 ■

LEMELSON
VINEYARDS

MEYER VINEYARD
PINOT NOIR
WILLAMETTE VALLEY

ALC. 14.1% BY VOL.

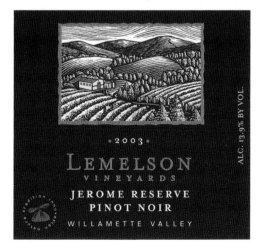

■ 2 0 0 3 ■

LEMELSON
VINEYARDS

JEROME RESERVE
PINOT NOIR
WILLAMETTE VALLEY

ALC. 13.9% BY VOL.

Carabella

2004 PINOT GRIS
WILLAMETTE VALLEY OREGON

ALC. 13.2% BY VOL

Autograph

ALCOHOL 13.9% BY VOLUME

R·STUART & C°.

2003 *Pinot Noir*

WILLAMETTE VALLEY
OREGON

ERATH

ESTATE SELECTION

willamette valley

PINOT NOIR   2002

750 ML

OREGON
PINOT NOIR

PRODUCED AND BOTTLED BY
KNUDSEN ERATH WINERY, DUNDEE, OREGON, USA OR BW-OR-52
ALC. 13% BY VOL.

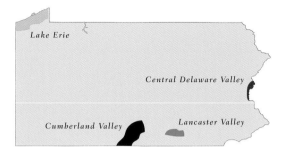

Pennsylvania

State Web site:
www.pennsylvaniawine.com

Number of wineries:
104

U.S. rank for number of wineries:
#7

First winery:
Franklin Hill Vineyard, 1982

Largest winery:
Chaddsford Winery

Well-known wineries:
Allegro Vineyards, Chaddsford Winery,
Pinnacle Ridge Winery

**American
viticultural areas:**
4—Central Delaware Valley, Cumberland Valley,
Lake Erie, Lancaster Valley

Acres of vines:
14,000 +

U.S. rank for acres of vines:
#4

TOP GRAPES:
Cabernet Sauvignon
Chardonnay
Gewürztraminer
Pinot Gris
Pinot Noir
Riesling

RHODE ISLAND

Southeastern New England

STATE WEB SITE:
www.american
wineries.org

**NUMBER OF
WINERIES:**
8

FIRST WINERY:
Sakonnet Vineyards, 1975

LARGEST WINERY:
Sakonnet Vineyards

AWARD-WINNING WINERY:
Sakonnet Vineyards

AMERICAN VITICULTURAL AREA:
1—Southeastern New England

ACRES OF VINES:
100 +

TOP GRAPES:
Chardonnay, Gewürztraminer, Pinot Noir

South Carolina

State Web site:
www.americanwineries.org

Number of wineries:
7

First winery:
Carolina Vineyards (formerly known as
Cruse Vineyards), 1985

Largest winery:
Irwin House Vineyards

Award-winning wineries:
Carolina Vineyards, Montmorenci Vineyards

American viticultural areas:
none

Acres of vines:
400 +

Top grapes:
Scuppernong, Chambourcin, Vidal Blanc

Montmorenci Vineyards

1999 Vintage **BLANC du BOIS** ALCOHOL 12.5% BY VOLUME
SOUTH CAROLINA TABLE WINE
Grown, Produced and Bottled by Montmorenci Vineyards
Aiken, South Carolina BW SC-14

SOUTH DAKOTA

STATE WEB SITE:
www.americanwineries.org

NUMBER OF WINERIES:
11

FIRST WINERY:
Valiant Vineyards Winery, 1996

LARGEST WINERY:
Valiant Vineyards Winery

WELL-KNOWN WINERIES:
Prairie Berry Winery, Valiant Vineyards Winery

AMERICAN VITICULTURAL AREAS:
none

ACRES OF VINES:
25 +

TOP GRAPES:
Baltica, Seyval Blanc, Maréchal Foch, Frontenac

Mississippi Delta

TENNESSEE

STATE WEB SITE:
www.tennesseewines.com

NUMBER OF WINERIES:
27

FIRST WINERY:
Highland Manor Winery, 1980

LARGEST WINERY:
Mountain Valley Vineyards

WELL-KNOWN WINERIES:
Beachaven Vineyards and Winery
Cordova Cellars

AMERICAN VITICULTURAL AREA:
1—Mississippi Delta

ACRES OF VINES:
196 +

TOP GRAPES:
Muscadine
Seyval Blanc
Chambourcin
Chardonnay

TENNESSEE VALLEY

Appalachian Red

PRODUCED AND BOTTLED BY
TENNESSEE VALLEY WINE CORPORATION
LOUDON, TN BW-TN-6
TABLE WINE CONTAINS SULFITES

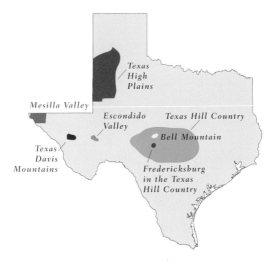

TEXAS

STATE WEB SITE:
www.americanwineries.org

NUMBER OF WINERIES:
101

U.S. RANK FOR NUMBER OF WINERIES:
#8

FIRST WINERY:
Val Verde Winery, 1883

LARGEST WINERY:
St. Genevieve Winery

WELL-KNOWN WINERIES:
Fall Creek Vineyards, Llano Estacado, Lost Creek
Vineyard and Winery, Spicewood Vineyards

AMERICAN VITICULTURAL AREAS:
7—Bell Mountain
Escondido Valley
Fredericksburg in the Texas Hill Country
Mesilla Valley
Texas Davis Mountains
Texas High Plains
Texas Hill Country

ACRES OF VINES:
2,900 +

TOP GRAPES:
Chenin Blanc, Chardonnay, Cabernet
Sauvignon, Merlot

UTAH

STATE WEB SITE:
www.americanwineries.org

NUMBER OF WINERIES:
7

FIRST WINERY:
Castle Creek Winery, 1989

LARGEST WINERY:
Castle Creek Winery

WELL-KNOWN WINERIES:
Castle Creek Winery, Spanish Valley Vineyards
and Winery

AMERICAN VITICULTURAL AREAS:
none

ACRES OF VINES:
20 +

TOP GRAPES:
Pinot Noir
Merlot
Cabernet Sauvignon
Chenin Blanc
Chardonnay
Gewürztraminer

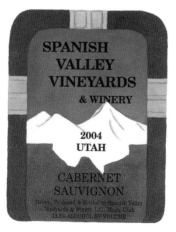

VERMONT

STATE WEB SITE:
www.americanwineries.org

NUMBER OF WINERIES:
9

FIRST WINERY:
Snow Farm Vineyard and Winery, 1985

LARGEST WINERY:
Boyden Valley Winery

WELL-KNOWN WINERIES:
North River Winery, Snow Farm Vineyard

AMERICAN VITICULTURAL AREAS:
none

ACRES OF VINES:
100 +

TOP GRAPES:
Seyval Blanc
Chardonnay
Baco Noir

VIRGINIA

STATE WEB SITE:
www.virginiawines.org

NUMBER OF WINERIES:
108

U.S. RANK FOR NUMBER OF WINERIES:
#5

FIRST WINERY:
Farfelu Vineyards, 1967

LARGEST WINERY:
Château Morrisette

WELL-KNOWN WINERIES:
AmRhein Wine Cellars
Barboursville Vineyards
Château Morrisette
Horton Vineyards
Keswick Vineyards
King Valley Vineyards
Kluge Estate Winery
Late Harvest Vidal
Rappahannock Cellars
Rockbridge Vineyard
White Hall Vineyards

AMERICAN VITICULTURAL AREAS:
6—Eastern Shore
Monticello
Northern Neck George Washington Birthplace
North Fork of Roanoke
Rocky Knob
Shenandoah Valley

ACRES OF VINES:
2,400 +

U.S. RANK FOR ACRES OF VINES:
#7

TOP GRAPES:
Chardonnay, Sauvignon Blanc,
Cabernet Sauvignon, Merlot, Norton

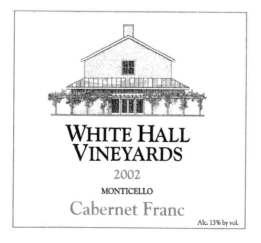

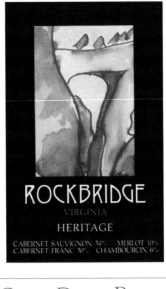

ROCKBRIDGE
VIRGINIA
HERITAGE

CABERNET SAUVIGNON 54%   MERLOT 10%
CABERNET FRANC 30%   CHAMBOURCIN 6%

OUR DOG BLUE

CHATEAU MORRISETTE

VIRGINIA HISTORIC LANDMARK

1814 BARBOURSVILLE RUINS
Designed by Thomas Jefferson

— 2003 —

VIRGINIA
VIOGNIER
RESERVE

Produced and Bottled by Barboursville Vineyards

ALCOHOL 13% BY VOL.

BARBOURSVILLE
Virginia

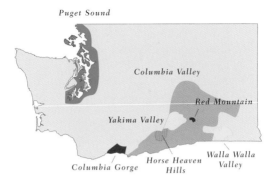

Puget Sound

Columbia Valley

Red Mountain

Yakima Valley

Horse Heaven Hills

Walla Walla Valley

Columbia Gorge

WASHINGTON

STATE WEB SITE:
www.washingtonwine.org

NUMBER OF WINERIES:
354

U.S. RANK FOR NUMBER OF WINERIES:
#2

FIRST WINERY:
Columbia Winery, 1962

LARGEST WINERY:
Château Ste. Michelle

WELL-KNOWN WINERIES:
See Chapter 5

AMERICAN VITICULTURAL AREAS:
7—Columbia Gorge
Columbia Valley
Horse Heaven Hills
Puget Sound
Red Mountain
Walla Walla Valley
Yakima Valley

ACRES OF VINES:
30,000 +

U.S. RANK FOR ACRES OF VINES:
#3

TOP GRAPES:
Merlot, Cabernet Sauvignon, Chardonnay,
Syrah, Riesling, Semillon

WOODWARD CANYON

2002

Walla Walla Valley
Estate Red Wine

ALC. 13.9% BY VOL.

CHARDONNAY
COLUMBIA VALLEY

Cold Creek
VINEYARD

Chateau Ste Michelle

HOGUE

JOHANNISBERG
RIESLING
Columbia Valley
2004

MCCREA
Cuvée Orleans
2002

Syrah

COLUMBIA·CREST
Grand Estates

COLUMBIA VALLEY
MERLOT

ALC 13 0% BY VOL

Sorella

COLUMBIA VALLEY

2002

L'Ecole Nº 41

2003
Seven Hills Vineyard • Walla Walla Valley
ESTATE SEMILLON

ALCOHOL 14.4% BY VOLUME

SEVEN HILLS

2001
CABERNET SAUVIGNON
WALLA WALLA VALLEY
SEVEN HILLS VINEYARD

ALCOHOL 13.5% BY VOLUME

CAYUSE
VINEYARDS

2002
SYRAH
Cailloux Vineyard
Walla Walla Valley

Alcohol 14.1% by vol.   750 ml

CANOE RIDGE
Vineyard

2003
Merlot
COLUMBIA VALLEY

Alc. 14.0% By Vol.

ESTATE GROWN

WEST VIRGINIA

STATE WEB SITE:
www.americanwineries.org

NUMBER OF WINERIES:
16

FIRST WINERY:
Fisher Ridge Winery, 1977

LARGEST WINERY:
Daniel Vineyards

AWARD-WINNING WINERIES:
Daniel Vineyards

AMERICAN VITICULTURAL AREAS:
3—Kanawha River Valley, Ohio River Valley,
Shenandoah Valley

ACRES OF VINES:
60 +

TOP GRAPES:
Niagara, Baco Noir, St. Vincent

WISCONSIN

STATE WEB SITE:
www.wiswine.com

NUMBER OF WINERIES:
32

FIRST WINERY:
Wollersheim Winery,
1972

LARGEST WINERY:
Simon Creek

**WELL-KNOWN
WINERIES:**
Botham Vineyards and
Winery, Von Stiehl
Winery

**AMERICAN
VITICULTURAL AREA:**
1—Lake Wisconsin

ACRES OF VINES:
80 +

TOP GRAPES:
Seyval Blanc
Riesling
Chardonnay
Pinot Noir

Lake Wisconsin

Wyoming

State Web site:
www.americanwineries.org

Number of wineries:
2

First winery:
Wyoming Craft and Wine Cellars, 1999

American viticultural areas:
none

Acres of vines:
15 +

Top grapes:
Merlot, Zinfandel

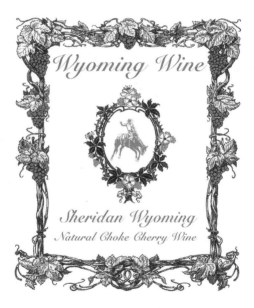

CHAPTER 5

The Wines of California, Washington, Oregon, and New York

Now that we have looked at the history and overview of American winemaking, let's turn our attention to the top four wine-producing states.

California

No wine-growing area in the world has come so far so quickly as California. Twenty years ago California wines were not necessarily considered worthy of comparison to European wines. Now, California wines are available worldwide, and shipments for export have increased dramatically over recent years to countries including Japan, Germany, and England.

California produces more than 90 percent of U.S. wine. California wines dominate American wine consumption, accounting for about 70 percent of all wine sales in the United States. Wine is also California's most valuable finished agricultural product, the industry generating $45 billion in annual revenues. By comparison, California's film industry generates $30 billion in revenues. If the state of California were a nation, it would be the fourth leading wine producer in the world!

An Introduction to California Wines

Viticultural Areas

The map on page 80 shows the important wine-making regions you should know. It's easier to remember them if you divide them into four groups:

North Coast: Napa County, Sonoma County, Mendocino County, Lake County (Best wines: Cabernet Sauvignon, Zinfandel, Sauvignon Blanc, Chardonnay, Merlot)

North Central Coast: Monterey County, Santa Clara County, Livermore County (Best wines: Syrah, Grenache, Viognier, Marsanne, Roussane, Chardonnay, Pinot Noir)

South Central Coast: San Luis Obispo County, Santa Barbara County (Best wines: Sauvignon Blanc, Chardonnay, Pinot Noir)

San Joaquin Valley: Known for jug wines

Napa Valley represents about 7 percent of California's wine production.

Acres of wine grapes planted in Napa: 42,929
Number of wineries: 250

Acres of wine grapes planted in Sonoma: 55,877
Number of wineries: 190

Although you may be most familiar with the names Napa and Sonoma, less than 12 percent of all California wine comes from these two regions combined. In fact, the bulk of California wine is produced in the San Joaquin Valley, mostly ordinary table wines, often referred to as jug wines. This region accounts for more than 50 percent of the wine grapes planted. Perhaps that makes California wine seem insignificant—that the production of jug wine dominates California wine-making history—but this is typical of most wine-producing countries. In France, for example, AOC wines account for only 35 percent of all French wines, while the rest are everyday table wines.

Last year, more than 15 million people visited California's wine growing areas. Vineyards and

A NOTE ON JUG WINES

The phrase *jug wines* refers to simple, uncomplicated, inexpensive, everyday drinking wine. You're probably familiar with these types of wine: They're sometimes labeled with a generic name, such as Chablis or Burgundy (even though they do not use any of the same grapes as the AOC wines from those regions in France). Inexpensive and well made, these wines were originally bottled in jugs, rather than in conventional wine bottles, hence the name: *jug wine*. They are very popular and account for the largest volume of California wine sold in the United States.

Ernest and Julio Gallo, who began their winery in 1933, are the major producers of jug wine in California. Many people credit the Gallo brothers with converting American drinking habits from spirits to wine. Some other wineries that produce jug wine are Almaden, Paul Masson, and Taylor California Cellars.

I believe the best-made jug wines in the world are from California. They maintain both consistency and quality from year to year.

wineries are the second most popular California tourist destination after Disneyland.

The Rise of Better Quality Wines

As early as the 1940s, Frank Schoonmaker, an importer and writer, and one of the first American wine experts, convinced some California winery owners to market their best wines using varietal labels, and transformed California's wine industry.

Robert Mondavi is an excellent example of a winemaker who has concentrated solely on varietal wine production. In 1966, Mondavi left his family's Charles Krug Winery and started the Robert Mondavi Winery. That major winery was among the first to switch to varietal labeling, which led to higher quality winemaking. "He was able to prove to the public what the people within the industry already knew—that California could produce world-class wines," said veteran winemaker Eric Wente. Mondavi's role was important to the evolution of varietal labeling of California wines.

There are many reasons for California's winemaking success, including:

Location: Napa and Sonoma counties, two of the most important regions for quality wine, are both less than a two-hour drive from San Francisco. This proximity encourages both residents and tourists to visit the regions' wineries, most of which offer wine tastings and sell their wines in their own shops.

Weather: Abundant sunshine, warm daytime temperatures, cool evenings, and a long growing season all add up to good conditions for growing many grape varieties. California is certainly subject to sudden changes in weather, but a fickle climate is not a major worry.

The University of California at Davis and Fresno State University: Throughout their history, both schools have been committed to developing outstanding schools of oenology and viticulture. Each has trained many young California winemakers, and their curricula—with their concentration on the scientific study of wine, viticulture, and, most important, technology—have world-class reputations. In fact, early California winemakers sent their children to study oenology at Geisenheim (Germany) or Bordeaux (France), while today many European winemakers send their children to these California institutions. Their research, focused on soil, different strains of yeast, hybridization, temperature-controlled fermentation, as well as many other viticultural techniques, has revolutionized the wine industry worldwide.

THE 20 TOP-SELLING CALIFORNIA WINES

1. Carlo Rossi (Gallo)
2. Franzia
3. Gallo Label
4. Gallo Reserve Cellars
5. Almaden
6. Inglenook
7. Sutter Home
8. Robert Mondavi
9. Beringer
10. Paul Masson
11. Glen Ellen
12. Vendange
13. Peter Vella
14. Fetzer
15. Sebastiani
16. Kendall-Jackson
17. William Wycliff
18. Taylor California
19. Blossom Hill
20. Turning Leaf (Gallo)

Money and Marketing Strategy: The important role of both money and marketing in the successful launch of any new wine cannot be overemphasized. Marketing may not create the wine, but it certainly helps sell it. As more and more winemakers concentrated on making the best wine they could, American consumers responded with enthusiasm. They were willing to buy—and pay—more as quality improved. In order to keep up with consumer expectations, winemakers realized that they needed more research, development, and—most important—working capital. The wine industry turned to investors, both corporate and individual.

Since 1967, when the now-defunct National Distillers bought Almaden, multinational corporations have recognized the profit potential of large-scale winemaking and have aggressively entered the wine business. They've brought huge financial resources and expertise in advertising and promotion that have helped assure the success of American wines both domestically and internationally. Other early corporate participants included Pillsbury, Coca-Cola, and even a company from Japan—Otsuka Pharmaceutical Company.

California Wine Style

Style refers to the characteristics of the grapes and of the wine itself, and is the individual winemaker's trademark as an "artist" who tries different techniques to explore the fullest potential of the grapes.

Most winemakers will tell you that 95 percent of winemaking begins with the quality of the grapes. The other 5 percent comes from the "personal touch" of the winemaker. It is also common for winemakers to move around from winery to winery, just as good chefs move from one restaurant to another. They often carry the same "recipe" from place to place, if it is particularly successful, and sometimes they experiment, creating new styles of wine.

Here are just a few of the hundreds of decisions a winemaker must make when developing his or her style of wine:

- When should the grapes be harvested?
- Should the juice be fermented in stainless-steel tanks or oak barrels? How long should it be fermented? At what temperature?
- Should the wine be aged at all? How long? If so, should it be aged in oak? What kind of oak—American, or French?
- What varieties of grape should be blended, and in what proportion?
- How long should the wine be aged in the bottle before it is sold?

And the list goes on. Because there are so many variables in winemaking, producers can create many styles of wine from the same grape variety—so you can choose the style that suits your taste. With the relative freedom of winemaking in the United States, the overall style of California wines continues to be diverse.

STAINLESS-STEEL FERMENTATION

Stainless-steel tanks are temperature controlled, which allows the winemakers to control the temperature at which the wine ferments. For example, a winemaker could ferment wines at a low temperature to retain fruitiness and delicacy, while preventing browning and oxidation.

Thinking about buying a vineyard in California?

Today, unplanted Napa Valley land costs between $100,000 and $200,000 per acre, requires an additional $20,000 per acre to plant, and will produce no income for three to five years. Add the cost of building a winery, buying equipment, and hiring the winemaker. In 2002, Francis Ford Coppola, owner of Niebaum-Coppola Wine Estate, paid a record price of $350,000 an acre for vineyard land in Napa.

One California wine country joke is this: "How do you make a small fortune in the wine business?" "Start with a large fortune and buy a winery."

The California Wine Conundrum

The renaissance of the California wine industry began only about forty years ago. Within that short period of time, some fourteen hundred new wineries have been established in California; today California lists more than sixteen hundred. Most of these wineries make more than one wine, in a range of styles and prices. For example, you can get a Cabernet Sauvignon wine ranging from "Two Buck Chuck" at $1.99 to Harlan Estate at more than $500 a bottle. Diversity, constant change, and experimentation all keep California winemaking in a state of flux.

California Varietal Wine Prices

You can't always equate quality with price. Some of the excellent varietal wines produced in California are well within the budget of the average consumer, although some varietals (primarily Chardonnay and Cabernet Sauvignon) may be quite expensive.

As in any market, supply and demand determine price. However, new wineries are burdened with high start-up costs, which are often reflected in the prices of their wines. Older, established wineries that have amortized their investments are often more reasonable and able to price their wines according to market forces of supply and demand. Remember, when you're buying California wine, price doesn't always reflect quality.

FROM THE CORPORATE LADDER TO THE VINE
Some of the pioneers of the back-to-the-land movement:

"FARMER"	WINERY	PROFESSION
Robert Travers	Mayacamas	Investment banker
David Stare	Dry Creek	Civil engineer
Tom Jordan	Jordan	Geologist
Rodney Strong	Rodney Strong	Dancer/ choreographer
James Barrett	Chateau Montelena	Attorney
Tom Burgess	Burgess	Air Force pilot
Jess Jackson	Kendall-Jackson	Attorney
Warren Winiarski	Stag's Leap	College professor
Brooks Firestone	Firestone	Take a guess!

Acadia
Alban
Altamura
Araujo
Arrowood
Artesa
David Arthur
Au Bon Climat
Beaulieu
Benziger Family
Beringer
Bernardus
Bond
Brander
David Bruce
Buehler
Burgess
Byron
Cakebread
Caldwell
Calera
Cardinale
Carlisle
Caymus
Chalk Hill
Chalone
Chappellet
Chateau Montelena
Chateau Potelle
Chateau St. Jean
Chateau Souverain
Chimney Rock
Clos du Bois
Clos du Val
B.R. Cohn
Conn Creek
Constant
Cornerstone
Robert Craig
Cuvaison
Dalla Valle
Del Dotto
Diamond Creek
Dolce
Domaine Carneros

Domaine Chandon
Dominus
The Donum Estate
Duckhorn
DuMol
Dunn
Dutton-Goldfield
Merry Edwards
Etude
Far Niente
Gary Farrell
Ferrari-Carano
Fisher
Flora Springs
Flowers
Foley Estate
Foppiano
Franciscan Oakville
Freemark Abbey
Gallo of Sonoma
Gemstone
Geyser Peak
Girard
Gloria Ferrer
Grgich Hills
Groth
Hanna
Hanzell
Harlan
Hartwell
HdV
Heitz
Hess Collection
Paul Hobbs
Hundred Acre
Iron Horse
J Vineyards & Winery
Jaffurs
Justin
Keller
Kendall-Jackson
Kathryn Kennedy
Kenwood
Kistler
Charles Krug

Kunde
Lagier Meredith
Lail
Landmark
Lang & Reed
Laurel Glen
Lewis
Lokoya
Loring
Luna
Markham
Marston Family
Matanzas Creek
Mendelson
Mer Soleil
Meridian
Merryvale
Peter Michael
Miner Family
Robert Mondavi
Morgan
Mueller
Mumm Cuvée Napa
Newton
Neyers
Nickel & Nickel
Niebaum-Coppola
Novy
Opus One
Pahlmeyer
Paloma
Patz & Hall
Peju Province
Joseph Phelps
Pine Ridge
Plumpjack
Pride Mountain
Provenance
Quintessa
Qupe
Ramey
Ravenswood
Martin Ray
Raymond
Renwood
Reverie
Ridge
Rochioli
Roederer Estate
Rosenbloom
Stephen Ross

Rudd
Rutherford Hill
St. Clement
St. Francis
St. Supery
Sanford
Saxum
Schramsberg
Screaming Eagle
Sebastiani
Seghesio
Selene
Sequoia Grove
Shafer
Siduri
Silver Oak
Silverado
Simi
Snowden
Sonoma Cutrer
Sonoma-Lobe
Spottswoode
Stag's Leap Wine Cellars
Stags' Leap Winery
Steele
Sterling
Stonestreet
Rodney Strong
Tablas Creek
Robert Talbott
Talley
Testarossa
Philip Togni
Tor Wines
Marimar Torres
Treana
Trefethen
Trinchero
Truchard
Verite
Villa Mt. Eden
Vine Cliff
Vision
Vlader
Whitehall Lane
Williams Selyem
Ken Wright

Choosing a California Wine

One reason California produces such a wide variety of wine is its many different climates. Some wine-growing areas are as cool as Burgundy, Champagne, and the Rhein, while others are as warm as the Rhône Valley, Portugal, and the southern regions of Italy and Spain. If that's not diverse enough, these wine-growing areas have inner districts with "microclimates," or climates within climates. One of the microclimates (which are among the designated AVAs) in Sonoma County, for example, is the Alexander Valley.

To better understand this concept, let's examine the Rudd label.

State: California
County: Sonoma
Viticultural Area (AVA):
Russian River Valley
Vineyard: Bacigalupi
Winery: Rudd

RUDD
Russian River Valley
BACIGALUPI VINEYARD
CHARDONNAY
2001
PRODUCED & BOTTLED BY RUDD
OAKVILLE, CALIFORNIA
ALCOHOL 14.5% BY VOLUME
750 ML.
Product of U.S.A.

California wine has no classification system that resembles the European AOC equivalent, but the labels tell you everything you need to know about the wine—and more. Here are some quick tips you can use when you scan the shelves at your favorite retailer. The label shown above will serve as an example.

The most important piece of information on the label is the producer's name. In this case, the producer is Rudd.

If the grape variety is on the label, a minimum of 75 percent of the wine must be derived from that grape variety. The Rudd label shows that the wine is made from the Chardonnay grape.

If the wine bears a vintage date, 95 percent of the grapes must have been harvested that year.

This wine label shows that most or all of the grapes were harvested in 2001.

If the wine is designated "California," then 100 percent of the grapes must have been grown in California.

If the label designates a certain federally recognized viticultural area (AVA), such as Russian River Valley (as on our example), then at least 85 percent of the grapes used to make that wine must have been grown in that location.

If an individual vineyard is noted on the label, 95 percent of the grapes must be from the named vineyard, which must be located within the approved AVA listed on the label.

The alcohol content is given in percentages. Usually, the higher the percentage of alcohol, the "fuller" the wine will be. This label shows that this wine has 14.5 percent alcohol.

"Produced and bottled by" means that at least 75 percent of the wine was fermented by the winery named on the label.

A 40-YEAR PERSPECTIVE

NUMBER OF BONDED WINERIES IN CALIFORNIA

YEAR	WINERIES
1965	232
1970	240
1975	330
1980	508
1985	712
1990	807
1995	944
2000	1,210
2005	1,600+

Source: *The Wine Institute*

Some wineries tell you the exact varietal content of the wine, and/or the sugar content of the grapes when they were picked, and/or the amount of residual sugar (to let you know how sweet or dry the wine is).

"Reserve" on the label has no legal meaning. In other words, there is no law that defines it. Some wineries, such as Beaulieu Vineyards and Robert Mondavi Winery, still mark some of their wines *Reserve*. BV's Reserve is from a particular vineyard. Mondavi's Reserve is made from a special blend of grapes, presumably their best. Others include Cask wines, Special Selections, or Proprietor's Reserve. The California Wine Institute has proposed a definition of Reserve to meet the requirement by some export markets.

THERE ARE 94 AVAs IN CALIFORNIA. SOME OF THE BEST KNOWN ARE:

Napa Valley

Sonoma Valley

Russian River Valley

Alexander Valley

Dry Creek Valley

Los Carneros

Anderson Valley

Santa Cruz Mountain

Livermore Valley

Paso Robles

Edna Valley

Fiddletown

Stag's Leap

Chalk Hill

Howell Mountain

Winemaking Techniques: California vs. European

European winemaking has established traditions that have remained essentially unchanged for hundreds of years. These practices involve the ways grapes are grown and harvested, and in some cases include winemaking and aging procedures.

In California there are few traditions, and winemakers are able to take full advantage of modern technology. Furthermore, there is freedom to experiment and create new products. Some of the California winemakers' experimentation, such as combining different grape varieties to make new styles of wine, is prohibited by some European wine-control laws. Californians thus have opportunities to try many new ideas—opportunities sometimes forbidden to European winemakers.

Another way in which California winemaking is different from European is that many California wineries carry an entire line of wine. Many of the larger wineries produce more than twenty different labels. In Bordeaux, most châteaux produce only one or two wines.

In addition to modern technology and experimentation, the fundamentals of wine growing can't be ignored: California's rainfall, weather pat-

---

FAMOUS INDIVIDUAL VINEYARDS OF CALIFORNIA

Bien Nacido	Martha's Vineyard
Dutton Ranch	McCrea
Durell	S.L.V.
Robert Young	To-Kalon
Bancroft Ranch	Beckstoffer
Geyserville	Monte Rosso
Gravelly Meadow	

terns, and soils are very different from those of Europe. The greater abundance of sunshine in California can result in wines with a greater alcohol content, ranging on average from 13.5 percent to 14.5 percent, compared to 12 percent to 13 percent on average in Europe. This higher alcohol content changes the balance and taste of the wines.

Devastation in the 1980s: The Return of Phylloxera

In the 1980s the plant louse phylloxera destroyed a good part of the vineyards in California, costing a billion dollars in new plantings. Now this may sound strange, but it proved that good can come from bad. So what's the good news?

This time, vineyard owners didn't have to wait to discover a solution; they already knew what they would have to do to replace the dead vines— by replanting with a different rootstock that they knew was resistant to phylloxera. So while the short-term effects were terribly expensive, the long-term result should be better quality wine.

In the early days of California grape growing, little thought was given to where a specific grape would grow best. Chardonnays were planted in climates that were much too warm, and Cabernet Sauvignons were planted in climates that were much too cold.

After the onset of phylloxera, winery owners were forced to rectify their errors, and, when replanting, they matched the climate and soil with the appropriate grape variety. Grape growers have also had the opportunity to plant different grape clones. The biggest change was in the planting density of the vines themselves. Traditional spacing used by most wineries before phylloxera was somewhere between 400 and 500 vines per acre.

Today with the new replanting, it is not uncommon to have more than a thousand vines per acre.

The bottom line is that if you like California wines now, you'll love them more with time. The quality is already better and the costs are lower—a win-win situation for everyone.

EUROWINEMAKING IN CALIFORNIA

Many well-known and highly regarded European winemakers have invested in California vineyards and are making their own wine. There are more than forty-five California wineries owned by European, Canadian, or Japanese companies, as well as many European wineries with operations in California. For example:

- One of the most influential joint ventures matched Baron Philippe de Rothschild, then the owner of Château Mouton-Rothschild in Bordeaux, and Robert Mondavi, of the Napa Valley, to produce a wine called Opus One.
- The owners of Château Pétrus in Bordeaux, the Moueix family, have vineyards in California. Their wine is a Bordeaux-style blend called Dominus.
- Moët & Chandon, which is part of Moët-Hennessy, owns Domaine Chandon in the Napa Valley.
- Roederer has grapes planted in Mendocino County and produces Roederer Estate.
- Mumm produces a sparkling wine, called Mumm Cuvée Napa.
- Taittinger has developed its own sparkling wine called Domaine Carneros.
- The Spanish sparkling-wine house Codorniu owns a winery called Artesa; and Freixenet owns land in Sonoma County and produces a wine called Gloria Ferrer.
- The Torres family of Spain owns a winery called Marimar Torres Estate in Sonoma County.
- Frenchman Robert Skalli (Fortant de France) owns more than six thousand acres in Napa Valley and the winery St. Supery.
- Tuscan wine producer Piero Antinori owns Atlas Peak winery in Napa.

Chardonnay—The Major White Grape Variety in California

There are more than twenty-four different varieties of white wine grapes grown in California, but the most important is Chardonnay (*Vitis vinifera*). This green-skinned grape is considered by many the finest white grape variety in the world. It is responsible for all the great French white Burgundies, such as Meursault, Chablis, and Puligny-Montrachet. In California, it has been the most successful white grape, yielding a wine of tremendous character and magnificent flavor. More than eight hundred different California Chardonnays are available to the consumer. The wines are often aged in small oak barrels, increasing their complexity. Because of their popularity, the grapes command high prices. Chardonnay is always dry and benefits from aging more than any other American white wine. Superior examples can keep and develop well in the bottle for five years or longer.

The Chardonnay Price Differential

You will find that a number of Chardonnays cost more than other varietals. As mentioned above, many wineries age these wines in wood—sometimes for more than a year. Oak barrels have doubled in price over the last five years, averaging six hundred dollars per barrel. Add to this the cost of the grapes and the length of time before the wine is actually sold, and you can see why the best of the California Chardonnays cost more than twenty-five dollars per bottle.

Variations in Taste

To explain the variety of different-tasting Chardonnays available, think of this: There are many brands of ice cream on the market. They use similar ingredients, but there is only one Ben & Jerry's. The same is true for wine. Among the many things to consider: Is a wine aged in wood or stainless steel? If wood, what type of oak? Was there barrel fermentation? Did the wine undergo a malolactic fermentation (conversion of malic acid to lactic acid in wine)? How long did the wine remain in the barrel (part of the style of the winemaker)? Where did the grapes come from?

Similarly, the aromas associated with Chardonnay have inspired descriptions ranging from apple, grapefruit, citrus, melon, and pineapple to butter, oak, toast, and vanilla.

Malolactic fermentation is a second fermentation that lowers tart malic acids and increases the softer lactic acids, making for a richer style wine. The result is what many wine tasters refer to as a buttery bouquet.

Kevin Zraly's Favorite Chardonnays

Acacia
Arrowood
Beringer
Cakebread
Chalk Hill
Chateau Montelena
Chateau St. Jean
Dutton Goldfield
Ferrari-Carano
Grgich Hills
Paul Hobbs
Kistler
Kongsgaard
Landmark
Marcassin
Martinelli
Peter Michael
Robert Mondavi
Phelps
Rudd Estate
Saintsbury
Silverado
Talbott

California Chardonnay
Best Bets

1997*
1999*
2000
2001*
2002*
2003*
2004
2005

Note: * signifies exceptional vintage

The two leading white table wines produced in the United States in 2005 were Chardonnay and Sauvignon Blanc/Fumé Blanc.

The Other Major California White Wine Grapes

Sauvignon Blanc

Sometimes labeled Fumé Blanc, this is one of the grapes used in making the dry white wines of the Graves region of Bordeaux and the white wines of Sancerre and Pouilly-Fumé in the Loire Valley of France, as well as in New Zealand. California Sauvignon Blanc makes one of the best dry white wines in the world. It is sometimes aged in small oak barrels and occasionally blended with the Sémillon grape. The aromas of Sauvignon Blanc have been described as grapefruit, grass, herbs, and cat pee.

KEVIN ZRALY'S FAVORITE SAUVIGNON BLANCS

Caymus
Chalk Hill
Chateau St. Jean
Dry Creek
Ferrari-Carano
Gainey
Mantanzas Creek
Mason
Robert Mondavi
Phelps
Silverado
Simi

Why is Sauvignon Blanc often labeled as Fumé Blanc? Robert Mondavi realized that no one was buying Sauvignon Blanc, so he changed its name to Fumé Blanc. Strictly a marketing maneuver—it was still the same wine. Result: Sales took off. To share his success, Mondavi decided not to trademark the name, so now anyone can use it (and many producers do).

Chenin Blanc

This is one of the most widely planted grapes in the Loire Valley of France. In California, the grape yields a very attractive, soft, light-bodied wine. It is usually made very dry or semi-sweet; it is a perfect apéritif wine, simple and fruity.

Viognier

One of the major white grapes from the Rhône Valley in France, Viognier thrives in warmer and sunny climates, so it's a perfect grape for the weather conditions in certain areas of California. It has a distinct fragrant bouquet. Not as full-bodied as most Chardonnays, nor as light as most Sauvignon Blancs, it's an excellent food wine.

Johannisberg Riesling

The true Riesling responsible for the best German wines of the Rhein and Mosel—and the Alsace wines of France—is also called White Riesling, or just Riesling. This grape produces white wine of distinctive varietal character in every style from bone-dry to very sweet dessert wines, which are often much better by themselves than with dessert. The smell of Riesling at its finest is always lively, fragrant, and both fruity and flowery.

Wine Trends

There has been a trend toward wineries specializing in particular grape varieties. Twenty years ago, I would have talked about which wineries in California were the best. Today, I'm more likely to talk about which winery or AVA makes the best Chardonnay; which winery makes the best Sauvignon Blanc; and the same would hold true for the reds, narrowing it down to who makes the best Cabernet Sauvignon, Pinot Noir, Merlot, Zinfandel, or Syrah.

The era of great experimentation with winemaking techniques is slowing down, and now the winemakers are making the finest possible wines they can from what they've learned in the 1980s and 1990s. I do expect to see some further experimentation to determine which grape varieties grow best in the various AVAs and microclimates. One of the biggest changes in the last twenty years is that wineries have also become more food-conscious in winemaking, adjusting their wine styles to go better with various kinds of food by lowering alcohol levels and increasing the acidity.

Chardonnay and Cabernet Sauvignon remain the two major grape varieties, but much more Syrah is being planted in California. Sauvignon Blanc (also called Fumé Blanc) wines have greatly improved; they're easier to consume young and while they still don't have the cachet of a Chardonnay, they are now better matched with most foods, I find. However, other white-grape varieties, such as Riesling and Chenin Blanc, aren't meeting with the same success, and they're harder to sell. Still, just to keep it interesting, some winemakers are planting more European varietals, such as Viognier.

Another significant development in California winemaking is the extent to which giant corporations have been buying up small, midsize, and even large wineries. The wine industry, like so many other businesses these days, has been subject to a great deal of consolidation as a result of mergers and acquisitions. See the list opposite for some notable examples of this trend.

Mergers and acquisitions:
A winery by any other name

Here, listed by the parent company, is a selection of some well-known wineries and brands.

Allied Domecq PLC

Atlas Peak, Buena Vista, Callaway Coastal Vineyards, Clos du Bois, William Hill, Mumm Napa

Beringer Blass (Foster's)

Beringer Vineyards, Carmenet, Chateau St. Jean, Chateau Souverian, Etude Wines, Meridian Vineyards, St. Clement, Stags' Leap Winery, Stone Cellars, Windsor

Constellation Brands, Inc.

Batavia Wine Cellars, Canandaigua Winery (includes Arbor Mist, J. Roget, Richards, Taylor), Columbia Winery, Covey Run Winery, Dunnewood Vineyards, Estancia Winery, Franciscan Vineyards, Mission Bell Winery (includes Almaden, Cook's Cribari, Inglenook, Le Domaine Paul Masson, Taylor California Cellars), Robert Mondavi Napa, Robert Mondavi Private Selection, Robert Mondavi Winery, Opus One, Woodbridge, Mount Veeder Winery, Quintessa, Ravenswood, Ste. Chapelle Winery, Simi Winery, Paul Thomas Winery, Turner Road Vintners (includes Heritage, La Terre, Nathanson Creek, Talus, Vendange)

Diageo

Beaulieu Vineyards, Blossom Hill, BV Coastal, The Monterey Vineyard, Painted Hills, Sterling Vineyards

Ernest and Julio Gallo

Anapamu Cellars, Frei Brothers Reserve, Gallo of Sonoma, Indigo Hills, MacMurray Ranch, Marcelina Vineyards, Louis M. Martini, Mirassou Vineyards, Rancho Zabaco, Redwood Creek, Turning Leaf

The Wine Group

Colony, Concannon, Corbett Canyon, Franzia, Glen Ellen, Lejon, Mogen David, Summit, M.G. Vallejo

Source: Wines & Vines 2004

MARGRIT BIEVER AND ROBERT MONDAVI:

With Chardonnay: oysters, lobster, a more complex fish with beurre blanc sauce, pheasant salad with truffles. With Sauvignon Blanc: traditional white meat or fish course, sautéed or grilled fish (as long as it isn't an oily fish).

FRANCIS MAHONEY (CARNEROS CREEK WINERY):

With Chardonnay: fowl, ham, and seafood in sauces. With Sauvignon Blanc: fish, turkey, shellfish, and appetizers.

DAVID STARE (DRY CREEK):

With Chardonnay: fresh boiled Dungeness crab cooked in Zatarain's crab boil, a New Orleans–style boil. Serve this with melted butter and a large loaf of sourdough French bread. With Sauvignon Blanc, "I like fresh salmon cooked in almost any manner. Personally, I like to take a whole fresh salmon or salmon steaks and cook them over the barbecue in an aluminum foil pocket. Place the salmon, onion slices, lemon slices, copious quantities of fresh dill, salt, and pepper on aluminum foil and make a pocket. Cook over the barbecue until barely done. Place the salmon in the oven to keep it warm while you take the juices from the aluminum pocket, reduce the juices, strain and whisk in some plain yogurt. Enjoy!"

WARREN WINIARSKI (STAG'S LEAP WINE CELLARS):

With Chardonnay: seviche, shellfish, salmon with a light hollandaise sauce.

JANET TREFETHEN (TREFETHEN VINEYARDS):

With Chardonnay: barbecued whole salmon in a sorrel sauce. With White Riesling: sautéed bay scallops with julienne vegetables.

RICHARD ARROWOOD (ARROWOOD VINEYARDS AND WINERY):

With Chardonnay: Sonoma Coast Dungeness crab right from the crab pot, with fennel butter as a dipping sauce.

BO BARRETT (CHATEAU MONTELENA WINERY):

With Chardonnay: salmon, trout, or abalone, barbecued with olive oil and lemon leaf and slices.

JACK CAKEBREAD (CAKEBREAD CELLARS):

"With my 2002 Cakebread Cellars Napa Valley Chardonnay: bruschetta with wild mushrooms, leek and mushroom–stuffed chicken breast, and halibut with caramelized endive and chanterelles."

ED SBRAGIA (BERINGER VINEYARDS):

With Chardonnay: lobster or salmon with lots of butter.

RODNEY STRONG (RODNEY STRONG):

With Chardonnay: Dover sole.

THE RED WINES OF CALIFORNIA

When I first began studying wines in 1970, peo-ple were more interested in red wine than white. From the mid-1970s, when I started teaching, into the mid-1990s, my students showed a defi-nite preference for white wine. Fortunately for me (since I am a red-wine drinker), the pendu-lum is surely swinging back to more red-wine drinkers. The chart below shows you the trend of wine consumption in the United States over the last thirty years.

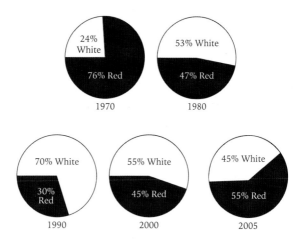

RED VS. WHITE—CONSUMPTION IN THE UNITED STATES

Looking back at the American obsession with health and fitness in the 1970s and 1980s, many people switched from meat and potatoes to fish and vegetables—a lighter diet that called more for white wine than red. "Chardonnay" became the new buzzword that replaced the call for "a glass of white wine." Bars that never used to stock wine—nothing decent, anyway—began to carry an assortment of fine wines by the glass, with

Chardonnay, by far, the best-selling wine. Today, steak is back and the new buzzwords are Cabernet Sauvignon and Syrah.

Another major reason for the dramatic upturn in red-wine consumption is the power of the media.

Finally, perhaps the most important reason that red wine consumption has increased in the United States is that California is producing a much better quality red wine than ever before. One of the reasons for improved quality is the replanting of vines over the last twenty years as a result of the phylloxera problem. Some analysts thought the replanting would be financially devastating to the California wine industry, but in reality it may have been a blessing in disguise, especially with regard to quality.

The opportunity to replant allowed vineyard owners to increase their red-grape production. It enabled California grape growers to utilize the knowledge they have gained over the years with regard to soil, climate, microclimate, trellising, and other viticultural practices. As a result, from 1991 to 2005, sales of red wine in all of the United States grew by more than 125 percent. Breaking California's acreage down further:

- Currently there are 288,262 acres in red grapes and 201,317 in white grapes planted in California.

- Napa is red wine country, with 27,000-plus acres in red grapes versus 11,000 acres in whites. Leading the red grapes is Cabernet Sauvignon, with 14,000 acres, while Chardonnay is the king of the whites with 9,000 acres.

- Bottom line: California reds are already some of the greatest in the world, with more and better to come.

The Major Red Grapes in California

While there are more than thirty red grape varieties planted in California, the top five red grapes are Cabernet Sauvignon, Zinfandel, Merlot, Pinot Noir, and Syrah.

Cabernet Sauvignon

Considered the most successful red grape in California, Cabernet Sauvignon yields some of the greatest red wines in the world. Cabernet is the predominant variety used in the finest red Bordeaux wines, such as Château Lafite-Rothschild and Château Latour. Almost all California Cabernets are dry, and depending upon the producer and vintage, they range in style from light and ready to drink to extremely full bodied and long lived. California Cabernet has become the benchmark for some of the best California wines.

Aromas that are typically characteristic of Cabernet Sauvignon are blackberry, cassis, black cherry, and eucalyptus. Most Cabernet Sauvignons are blended with other grapes, primarily Merlot. To include the grape variety on the label, however, the winemaker must use at least 75 percent Cabernet Sauvignon.

THE FRENCH PARADOX

In the mid-1990s, the TV series *60 Minutes* twice aired a report on a phenomenon known as the French Paradox—the fact that the French have a lower rate of heart disease than Americans, despite a diet that's higher in fat. Since the one thing the American diet lacks, in comparison to the French diet, is red wine, some researchers were looking for a link between the consumption of red wine and a decreased rate of heart disease. Not surprisingly, in the year following this report, Americans increased their purchases of red wines by 39 percent.

KEVIN ZRALY'S FAVORITE CALIFORNIA CABERNET SAUVIGNONS:

Arrowood
Beaulieu Private Reserve
Beringer Private Reserve
Cakebread
Caymus Special Selection
Chateau Montelena
Chateau St. Jean, Cinq Cepages
Dalla Valle
Diamond Creek
Duckhorn
Dunn Howell Mountain
Gallo of Sonoma Estate
Groth Reserve
Heitz
Hess Collection
Paul Hobbs
Jordan
Joseph Phelps
La Jota
Laurel Glen
Louis Martini
Mondavi Reserve
Opus One
Pine Ridge
Pride Mountain
Ridge Monte Bello
Shafer Hillside Select
Silver Oak
Spottswood
Staglin
Stag's Leap Cask
Whitehall Lane

THE HESS
COLLECTION
MOUNT VEEDER
NAPA VALLEY CABERNET SAUVIGNON
2001

1994*
1995*
1996*
1997*
1999*
2000
2001*
2002*
2003*
2004
2005

Note: * signifies exceptional vintage

Pinot Noir

Known as the "headache" grape because of its fragile quality, Pinot Noir is temperamental, high-maintenance, expensive, and difficult to grow and make into wine. The great grape of the Burgundy region of France—responsible for such famous wines as Gevrey-Chambertin, Nuits-St-Georges, and Pommard—is also one of the principal grapes in French Champagne. In California, many years of experimentation in finding the right location to plant Pinot Noir and to perfect the fermentation techniques have elevated some of the Pinot Noirs to the status of great wines. Pinot Noir is usually less tannic than Cabernet and matures more quickly, generally in two to five years. Because of the extra expense involved in growing this grape, the best examples of Pinot Noirs from California may cost more than other varietals.

Southern California—especially the Santa Barbara area, as the characters in *Sideways* could tell you—has become one of the prime locations for Pinot Noir production, with plantings up by more than 200 percent in the past decade. In fact, Pinot Noir sales overall have increased at least 20 percent since the film came out. The Carneros district, in the North Coast, is also one of the better places to grow Pinot Noir because of its cooler climate. Common Pinot Noir aromas are red berries, red cherry, leather, and tobacco for older Pinots.

KEVIN ZRALY'S FAVORITE CALIFORNIA PINOT NOIRS:

Acacia

Artesa

Au Bon Climat

Calera

Carneros Creek

Cline

Dehlinger

Merry Edwards

Etude

Gary Farrell

Flowers

Paul Hobbs

Marcassin

Robert Mondavi

Morgan

Ramey

J. Rochioli

Saintsbury

Sanford

Williams Selyem

One author, trying to sum up the difference between a Pinot Noir and a Cabernet Sauvignon, said, "Pinot is James Joyce, while Cabernet is Dickens. Both sell well, but one is easier to understand."

1999
2000
2001*
2002*
2003*
2004

Note: * signifies exceptional vintage

Zinfandel

The surprise grape of California, Zinfandel was used to make "generic" or jug wines in the early years of California winemaking. Over the past twenty years, however, it has developed into one of the best red varietal grapes. The only problem in choosing a Zinfandel wine is that so many different styles are made. In the 2002 vintage, Turley winery made eighteen different Zinfandels. Depending on the producer, the wines can range from a big, rich, ripe, high alcohol, spicy, smoky, concentrated, intensely flavored style with substantial tannin, to a very light, fruity wine. And let's not forget white Zinfandel! Some Zinfandels have more than 16 percent alcohol. Recent DNA studies have concluded that Zinfandel is the same grape as the Primitivo in Italy.

One of the hottest wines today in terms of popularity is white Zinfandel, which at 35 million cases sold in 2003 far outsells red Zinfandel. It is also the largest-selling varietal wine in the United States.

BEST BETS FOR ZINFANDEL

1994*
1995*
1997*
1999*
2001
2002*
2003*
2004
2005

*Note: * signifies exceptional vintage*

KEVIN ZRALY'S FAVORITE ZINFANDELS:

Carlisle
Cline
Dry Creek
Merry Edwards
Fife
Rafanelli
Ravenswood
Ridge
J. Rochioli
Rosenblum
Roshambo
St. Francis
Seghesio
Signorello
Turley

Merlot

In the early years of California winemaking, Merlot was thought of as a grape only to be blended with Cabernet Sauvignon, because Merlot's tannins are softer and its texture is more supple. Merlot has now achieved its own identity as a superpremium varietal. Of red grape varietals in California, Merlot saw the fastest rate of new plantings over the last twenty years. It produces a soft, round wine that generally does not need the same aging as a Cabernet Sauvignon. It is a top seller at restaurants, where its early maturation and compatibility with food make it a frequent choice by consumers.

There were only two acres of Merlot planted in all of California in 1960. Today there are more than fifty thousand!

Common Merlot aromas are blackberry, cassis, cherry, chocolate, coffee, and oak.

BEST BETS FOR MERLOT

1994*
1997*
1999*
2001*
2002*
2003*
2004
2005

*Note: * signifies exceptional vintage*

KEVIN ZRALY'S FAVORITE MERLOTS:

Beringer Howell Mountain
Chimney Rock
Clos du Bois
Duckhorn
Franciscan
Havens
Lewis Cellars
Markham
Matanzas Creek
Newton
Phelps
Pine Ridge
Pride
Provenance
St. Francis
Shafer
Whitehall Lane

Syrah

The up-and-coming red grape in California is definitely Syrah. I don't know why it's taken so long, since Syrah has always been one of the major grapes of the Rhône Valley in France, making some of the best and most long-lived wines in the world. Further, the sales of Australian Syrah (which they call Shiraz) have been phenomenal in the United States. Americans like the spicy, robust flavor of this grape. It's a perfect grape for California because it thrives in sunny, warm weather.

KEVIN ZRALY'S FAVORITE SYRAHS:

Alban
Cakebread
Clos du Bois
Edmunds St. John
Fess Parker
Geyser Park
Lewis
Ojai
Phelps
Qupe
Wild Horse
Zaca Mesa

BEST BETS FOR SYRAH

2002*
2003*
2004
2005

*Note: * signifies exceptional vintage*

Red-Grape Boom

Look at the chart below to see how many acres of the major red grapes were planted in California in 1970, and how those numbers have increased. Rapid expansion has been the characteristic of the California wine industry!

TOTAL BEARING ACREAGE OF RED-WINE GRAPES PLANTED GRAPE-BY-GRAPE COMPARISON

GRAPE	1970	1980	1990	2005
Cabernet Sauvignon	3,200	21,800	24,100	75,994
Merlot	100	2,600	4,000	52,190
Zinfandel	19,200	27,700	28,000	50,381
Pinot Noir	2,100	9,200	8,600	23,879
Syrah			400	16,054

Meritage Wines

Meritage (which rhymes with "heritage") is the name for red and white wines made in America from a blend of the classic Bordeaux wine-grape varieties. This category was created because many winemakers felt stifled by the required minimum amount (75 percent) of a grape that must go into a bottle for it to be named for that variety. Some winemakers knew they could make a better wine with a blend of, say, 60 percent of the major grape and 40 percent secondary grapes. This blending of grapes allows producers of Meritage wines the same freedom that Bordeaux winemakers have in making their wines. For red wine, the varieties include Cabernet Franc, Cabernet Sauvignon, Malbec, Merlot, and Petit Verdot. For white wine, the varieties include Sauvignon Blanc and Sémillon. Some examples of Meritage wines of California:

Cain Five

Cinq Cepages (Chateau St. Jean)

Dominus (Christian Moueix)

Insignia (Phelps Vineyards)

Magnificat (Franciscan)

Opus One (Mondavi/Rothschild)

OPUS ONE

Opus One was the brainchild of Baron Philippe de Rothschild, proprietor of first-growth Château Mouton Rothschild in Pauillac, Bordeaux, and Robert Mondavi, Napa Valley's creative visionary winemaker. Launched in 1984, Opus One created its own niche as the premiere "ultra-premium" wine. "It isn't Mouton and it isn't Mondavi," said Robert Mondavi. Opus One is a Bordeaux-style blend made from Cabernet Sauvignon, Merlot, and Cabernet Franc grapes grown in Napa Valley. It was originally produced at the Robert Mondavi Winery in Napa Valley but is now produced across Highway 29 in its own spectacular winery.

Wine collectors started a frenzy by buying Cabernet Sauvignon from small California wineries at extraordinary prices. These "cult" wineries produce very little wine—with hefty price tags.

Araujo	4,000 cases
Dalla Valle	2,500 cases
Harlan Estate	1,800 cases
Bryant Family	1,000 cases
Screaming Eagle	500 cases
Colgin Cellars	400 cases
Grace Family	48 cases

Wine Styles

When you buy a Cabernet, Zinfandel, Merlot, Pinot Noir, Syrah, or Meritage wine there is no one way to determine which style of that wine you are getting. Style is not indicated on the label. Unless you just happen to be familiar with a particular vineyard's wine, you're stuck with trial-and-error tastings. You're one step ahead, though, just by knowing that you'll find drastically different styles from the same grape variety.

With more than sixteen hundred wineries in California and more than half of them producing red wines, it is virtually impossible to keep up with the ever-changing styles that are being produced. One of the recent improvements in labeling is that more wineries are adding such important information to the back label—when the wine is ready to drink, whether it should be aged, and even suggestions for food pairings.

To avoid any unpleasant surprises, I can't emphasize enough the importance of an educated wine retailer. One of the strongest recommendations I give—especially to a new wine drinker—is to find the right retailer, one who understands wine and your taste.

One of the most memorable tastings I have ever attended in my career was for the fiftieth anniversary of Beaulieu's Private Reserve wine. Over a two-day period, we tasted every vintage from 1936 to 1986 with winemaker André Tchelistcheff. I think everyone who attended the tasting was amazed and awed by how well many of these vintages aged.

Aging California Reds

California reds, especially from the best wineries that produce Cabernet Sauvignon and Zinfandel, age well. I have been fortunate to taste some early examples of Cabernet Sauvignon going back to the 1930s, 1940s, and 1950s, which for the most part were drinking well—some of them outstanding—proving to me the longevity of certain Cabernets. Cabernet Sauvignon and Zinfandel from the best wineries in great vintages will need a minimum of five years before you drink them, and they will get better over the next ten years. That's at least fifteen years of great enjoyment.

However, one of the things I have noticed in the last ten years, not only tasting as many California wines as I have, but also tasting so many European wines, is that California wines seem to be more accessible when young, as opposed to, say, a Bordeaux. I believe this is one of the reasons California wines sell so well in retail stores and in restaurants. I also have found, however, that most California Cabernets do not have the same ability to age over twenty years as do the best wines from Bordeaux.

Red Wine Trends

Red wines from California have traversed much terrain over the last thirty or so years. As time has passed there have been notable agricultural, technical, and stylistic developments in the industry. The 1960s were a decade of expansion and development. The 1970s were about growth, especially in terms of the number of wineries that were established in California and the corporations and individuals that became involved. The 1980s and 1990s were the decades of experimentation, in grape growing as well as in winemaking and marketing techniques.

Over the past ten years, I have seen winemakers finally get a chance to step back and fine-tune their wine. Today, they are producing wines that have tremendous structure, finesse, and elegance—characteristics that many wines lacked in the early years of the California winemaking renaissance. The benchmark for quality has increased to such a level that the best wineries have gotten better, but more important to the consumer, even everyday wines (under fifteen dollars) are better than ever before.

Though California winemakers have settled down, they have not given up experimentation altogether, if you consider the many new grape varieties coming out of California these days. I expect to see more wines made with grapes such as the Mourvèdre, Grenache, Sangiovese, and especially Syrah continuing the trend toward diversity in California red wines.

Red wines are no longer the sole domain of Napa and Sonoma. Many world-class reds are being produced in the Central Coast regions of California such as Monterey and Santa Barbara, San Luis Obispo, and Santa Clara.

Margrit Biever and Robert Mondavi (Robert Mondavi Winery):

With Cabernet Sauvignon: lamb, or wild game such as grouse and caribou. With Pinot Noir: pork loin, milder game such as domestic pheasant, coq au vin.

Tom Jordan (Jordan Vineyard and Winery):

"Roast lamb is wonderful with the flavor and complexity of Cabernet Sauvignon. The wine also pairs nicely with sliced breast of duck, and grilled squab with wild mushrooms. For a cheese course with mature Cabernet, milder cheeses, such as young goat cheeses, St. André and Taleggio, are best so the subtle flavors of the wine can be enjoyed."

Margaret and Dan Duckhorn (Duckhorn Vineyards):

"With a young Merlot, we recommend lamb shanks with crispy polenta, or grilled duck with wild rice in Port sauce. One of our favorites is barbecued leg of lamb with a mild, spicy fruit-based sauce. With older Merlots at the end of the meal, we like to serve cambazzola cheese and warm walnuts."

Janet Trefethen (Trefethen Vineyards):

With Cabernet Sauvignon: prime cut of well-aged grilled beef; also—believe it or not—with chocolate and choco-late-chip cookies. With Pinot Noir: roasted quail stuffed with peeled kiwi fruit in a Madeira sauce. Also with pork tenderloin in a fruity sauce.

Paul Draper (Ridge Vineyards):

With Zinfandel: a well-made risotto of Petaluma duck. With aged Cabernet Sauvignon: Moroccan lamb with figs.

Warren Winiarski (Stag's Leap Wine Cellars):

With Cabernet Sauvignon: lamb or veal with a light sauce.

Josh Jensen (Calera Wine Co.):

"Pinot Noir is so versatile, but I like it best with fowl of all sorts—chicken, turkey, duck, pheasant, and quail, preferably roasted or mesquite grilled. It's also great with fish such as salmon, tuna, and snapper."

Richard Arrowood (Arrowood Vineyards and Winery):

With Cabernet Sauvignon: Sonoma County spring lamb or lamb chops prepared in a rosemary herb sauce.

David Stare (Dry Creek Vineyard):

"My favorite food combination with Zinfandel is marinated, butterflied leg of lamb. Have the butcher butterfly the leg, then place it in a plastic bag. Pour in half a bottle of Dry Creek Zinfandel, a cup of olive oil, six mashed garlic cloves, and salt and pepper to taste. Marinate for several hours or overnight in the refrigerator. Barbecue until medium rare. While the lamb is cooking, take the marinade, reduce it, and whisk in several pats of butter for thickness. Yummy!"

Bo Barrett (Chateau Montelena Winery):

With Cabernet Sauvignon: a good rib eye, barbecued with a teriyaki-soy-ginger-sesame marinade, venison or even roast beef prepared with olive oil and tapenade with rosemary, or even lamb. But when it comes to a good Cabernet Sauvignon, Bo is happy to enjoy a glass with "nothing at all—just a good book."

Patrick Campbell (Laurel Glen Vineyard):

"With Cabernet Sauvignon, try a rich risotto topped with wild mushrooms."

Jack Cakebread (Cakebread Cellars):

"I enjoy my 1994 Cakebread Cellars Napa Valley Cabernet Sauvignon with farm-raised salmon with a crispy potato crust or an herb-crusted Napa Valley rack of lamb, with mashed potatoes and a red wine sauce."

Ed Sbragia (Beringer Vineyards):

"I like my Cabernet Sauvignon with rack of lamb, beef, or rare duck."

Tom Mackey (St. Francis Merlot):

With St. Francis Merlot Sonoma County: Dungeness crab cakes, rack of lamb, pork roast, or tortellini. With St. Francis Merlot Reserve: hearty minestrone or lentil soup, venison, or filet mignon, or even a Caesar salad.

WASHINGTON STATE

In Washington, the climatic conditions are a little cooler and rainier than in California, but it's neither too cold nor too wet to make great wine. The winegrowing regions are protected from Washington's famous rains by the Cascade Mountains. The earliest record of grape growing in Washington can be traced back to 1825, while the beginning of its modern winemaking industry can be dated to 1967, with the first wine produced under the Chateau Ste. Michelle label.

The four major white grapes grown in Washington are Chardonnay, Riesling, Gewürztraminer, and Sauvignon Blanc. Washington State has more Riesling planted than any other state in the United States. In the 1960s and 1970s, Washington was known only for white wines, but now it has become known as one of the great American states for the production of red wines, especially Merlot and Cabernet Sauvignon. (As it turns out, the state's Columbia Valley is on the same latitude as Bordeaux, France). Over the last ten years Washington winemakers have increased their plantings of Syrah, and the recent vintages are turning out to be of very high quality. In 2004, Washington State's wine production was 57 percent red versus 43 percent white.

There are six AVAs: Columbia Gorge, Columbia Valley, Puget Sound, Red Mountain, Walla Walla, and Yakima.

AVA (Date AVA established)	Number of Wineries
Yakima (1983)	40
Walla Walla (1984)	55
Columbia Valley* (1984)	150+
Puget Sound (1995)	35
Red Mountain (2001)	10
Columbia Gorge (2004)	8

* Largest viticultural area, responsible for 95 percent of production.

In 1990 in Washington, there were fewer than 70 wineries, which turned out less than 2 million cases. Acreage has increased from 10,000 acres to more than 30,000. Some of the wineries to look for include Canoe Ridge; Cayuse; Chateau Ste. Michelle, Washington's largest winery; Columbia Crest; Columbia Winery; Hogue Cellars; L'Ecole No. 41; Leonetti Cellars; McCrea Cellars; Quilceda Creek; Seven Hills; Andrew Will; and Woodward Canyon Winery.

Chateau Ste. Michelle has formed a winemaking partnership with the famous German wine producer Dr. Loosen. The new Riesling wine is called Eroica.

WASHINGTON BEST BETS

2001*
2002*
2004*

Note: * signifies exceptional vintage

Vital statistics

Oregon

11,100 acres, 240 wineries

Washington

More than 30,000 acres, 354 wineries

New York

31,000 acres, 212 wineries

Napa Valley

42,929 acres, 250 wineries

Oregon

Although grapes were planted and wine was made as early as 1847 in Oregon, the modern era began in the early 1960s. Today, Oregon, because of its climate, is becoming well known for Burgundian-style wines. By *Burgundian*-style I'm referring to Chardonnay and Pinot Noir, which are the major grapes planted in Oregon. Many critics feel the best Pinot Noir grown in the United States is from Oregon, with the 2002 vintage being its best ever. Another success in Oregon is Pinot Gris (aka Pinot Grigio), which has recently overtaken Chardonnay as the most widely planted white grape in the state. The largest producer of Pinot Gris (Grigio) in the United States is King Estate in Oregon.

The major AVA in Oregon is the Willamette Valley, near Portland. About 70 percent of Oregon's wineries are located there. Other AVAs include Applegate Valley, Rogue Valley, and Umpqua. Two others, the Columbia Valley and Walla Walla, are AVAs of both Oregon and Washington State.

Oregon best bets

1999*

2001

2002**

2003

2004*

*Note: * signifies exceptional vintage*
*** one of the best vintages ever for Pinot Noir in Oregon*

Wineries to look for include:

Adelsheim	Eyrie Vineyards
Archery Summit	King Estate
Argyle	Ponzi Vineyards
Beaux Frères	Rex Hill
Bergström	Sokol Blosser
Bethel Heights	Tualatin
Cristom	St. Innocent
Domaine Serene	Ken Wright
Erath	

Also, the famous Burgundy producer Joseph Drouhin owns a winery in Oregon called Domain Drouhin, producing, not surprisingly, Burgundy-style wines.

New York State

New York is the third largest wine-producing state in the United States, with eight AVAs and more than two hundred wineries. The three premium wine regions are:

Finger Lakes (73 wineries): With the largest wine production east of California.

Hudson Valley (28 wineries): Comprised mostly of premium farm wineries. This is one of America's oldest wine-growing regions: Grapevines were planted by the French Huguenots in the 1600s. It also boasts the oldest active winery in the United States—Brotherhood, which recorded its first vintage in 1839.

Long Island (33 wineries): New York's fastest-growing wine region. The climate on Long Island has more than two hundred days of sunshine and a long growing season, making it perfect for Merlot and Bordeaux-style wines. Its three AVAs are the Hamptons, Long Island, and North Fork. The first winery on Long Island was started in 1973 by Alex and Louisa Hargrave. Since 1995, vine-planted acreage on the North Fork has doubled, and production has surpassed 500,000 cases of wine.

Today, more than 80 of the 212 New York State wineries produce *vinifera* wines. Examples of *Vitis vinifera* grapes are Cabernet Sauvignon, Chardonnay, Merlot, Pinot Grigio, Pinot Noir, Riesling, Sauvignon Blanc, and Syrah.

There are three main categories:
Native American (*Vitis labrusca*)
European (*Vitis vinifera*)
French-American (hybrids)

Native American Varieties

The *Vitis labrusca* grapes are very popular among grape growers in New York because they are hardy and can withstand cold winters. Among the most familiar grapes of the *Vitis labrusca* family are Concord, Catawba, and Delaware. Until the last decade, these were the grapes used to make most New York wines. In describing these wines, words such as foxy, grapey, Welch's, and Manischewitz are often used. These words are a sure sign of *Vitis labrusca*.

European Varieties

Forty years ago, some New York wineries began to experiment with the traditional European (*Vitis vinifera*) grapes. Dr. Konstantin Frank, a Russian viticulturist skilled in cold-climate grape growing, came to the United States and catalyzed efforts to grow *Vitis vinifera* in New York. This was unheard of—and laughed at—back then. Other vintners predicted that he'd fail, that it was impossible to grow *vinifera* in New York's cold and capricious climate.

"What do you mean?" Dr. Frank replied. "I'm from Russia—it's even colder there."

Most people were still skeptical, but Charles Fournier of Gold Seal Vineyards was intrigued enough to give Dr. Frank a chance to prove his theory. Sure enough, Dr. Frank was successful with the *vinifera* and has produced some world-class wines, especially his Riesling and Chardonnay. So have many other New York wineries, thanks to the vision and courage of Dr. Frank and Charles Fournier.

French-American Varieties

Some New York and East Coast winemakers have planted French-American hybrid varieties, which combine European taste characteristics with American vine hardiness to withstand the cold winters in the Northeast. These varieties were originally developed by French viticulturists in the nineteenth century. Seyval Blanc and Vidal are the most prominent white wine varieties; Baco Noir and Chancellor are the most common reds.

Trends in New York State Wines

The most significant developments are taking place on Long Island, which has experienced the fastest growth of new vineyards. In the last twenty years, its grape-growing acreage has increased from one hundred acres to more than three thousand acres, with more expansion expected in the future.

The predominant use of *Vitis vinifera* varieties allows Long Island wineries to compete more effectively in the world market, and Long Island's longer growing season offers greater potential for red grapes.

The Millbrook Winery in the Hudson Valley has shown that this region can produce world-class wines—not only white, but red too, from such grapes as Pinot Noir and Cabernet Franc.

The wines of the Finger Lakes region continue to get better as the winemakers work with grapes that thrive in the cooler climate, including European varieties such as Chardonnay, Pinot Noir, and Riesling.

WINERIES TO LOOK FOR IN NEW YORK STATE:

THE FINGER LAKES

Dr. Konstantin Frank
Fox Run
Glenora
Standing Stone
Wagner
Herman Weimer

THE HUDSON VALLEY

Benmarl
Clinton Vineyards
Millbrook

LONG ISLAND

Bedell
Castello di Borghese (Hargrave)
Channing Daughters
Galluccio Estates
Lenz
Palmer
Paumanok
Pindar
Pellegrini
Schneider
Wölffer

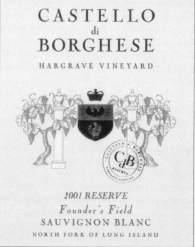

CASTELLO
di
BORGHESE

HARGRAVE VINEYARD

2001 RESERVE
Founder's Field
SAUVIGNON BLANC
NORTH FORK OF LONG ISLAND

Kevin Zraly's Best Picks

I TASTE MORE THAN three thousand wines a year, most of them blind tastings, and one of the great joys of wine tasting is the surprise of giving a high rating to an inexpensive wine. Over the years, I have found certain wineries in the United States that consistently produce great wines at great prices.

Here is a list of my picks for "Best Value American Wines" and my choices for "Under $50 but Worth the Money." Most of these wines are available at retail outlets throughout the country.

As you will note, nearly all of these wines are produced in California, with the rest from Washington and Oregon.

I have been fortunate, while traveling around the country, to try Valiant Vineyards from South Dakota, Harperfield from Ohio, Gruet from New Mexico, Dos Cabezas from Arizona, Ste. Chapelle from Idaho, Shelton Vineyards from North Carolina, Chaddsford from Pennsylvania, Kluge from Virginia, Fall Creek from Texas, and hundreds of other great American wines that are not from the "big four" states.

I look forward to a time when I can recommend terrific wines from all fifty states, but for now, because of the complexity of state-by-state alcohol regulations, these other wines are simply not available to consumers on any dependable basis. I would love to have included even my own home state of New York in the list below, but alas, the lack of national distribution for even the better New York State wines makes them difficult to find. For now, you either have to visit the winery or purchase them in a restaurant or retail store in the state. With the new Supreme Court ruling in favor of interstate shipping, I hope that states will soon revise their laws, paving the way for many of these delightful wines to be shipped from the winery to your home.

Best Values

California

Amberhill Cabernet Sauvignon

Beaulieu Merlot Costal

Benziger Chardonnay, Merlot, or Cabernet Sauvignon

Beringer Chardonnay and Merlot Founders-Estate

Buena Vista Sauvigon Blanc

Carmenet Cabernet Sauvignon

Chateau St. Jean Chardonnay and Sauvignon Blanc

Chateau Souverain Chardonnay

Chateau Souverain Merlot

Cline Cellars Zinfandel

Eschol Cabernet and Chardonnay

Estancia Chardonnay or Cabernet Sauvignon

Ferrari-Carano Fume Blanc

Fetzer Barrel Select Cabernet, Sauvignon, or Zinfandel

Fetzer Sundial Chardonnay and Merlot Eagle Peak

Forest Glen Merlot, Cabernet Sauvignon or Shiraz

Forest Ville Selections Cabernet or Chardonnay

Frog's Leap Sauvignon Blanc

Gallo of Sonoma Chardonnay, Cabernet Sauvignon, Pinot Noir, and Merlot

Geyser Peak Sauvignon Blanc

Hawk Crest Chardonnay, Cabernet Sauvignon, or Merlot

Kendall-Jackson Chardonnay Vintners Reserve, Syrah, or Cabernet Sauvignon

Laurel Glen Quintana Cabernet Sauvignon

Liberty School Cabernet Sauvignon

Markham Merlot and Sauvignon Blanc

Mason Sauvignon Blanc

Meridian Chardonnay or Cabernet Sauvignon

Robert Mondavi Woodbridge Selections

Monterey Vineyard Cabernet Sauvignon

Napa Ridge Merlot

Ravenswood Zinfandel Napa Valley

R.H. Phillips Cabernet Sauvignon Barrel Cuvee

Ridge Zinfandel (Sonoma)

Rosenblum Zinfandel Vintners Cuvee

Round Hill Chardonnay

St. Francis Merlot

St. Supery Sauvignon Blanc

Saintsbury Chardonnay

Sebastiani Chardonnay, Sonoma

Silverado Sauvignon Blanc

Simi Cabernet Sauvignon

Simi Sauvignon Blanc or Chardonnay

WASHINGTON STATE

Canoe Ridge Merlot

Chateau St. Michelle Riesling Eroica

Columbia Crest Chardonnay, Merlot, Cabernet Sauvignon, and Semillon-Chardonnay

Covey Run Fume Blanc, Chardonnay and Merlot

Hogue Chardonnay Columbia Valley

Hogue Fumé Blanc, Cabernet Sauvignon, or Merlot

Under $50 but Worth the Money

California

Cabernet Sauvignon

Artesa

Beaulieu Rutherford

Beringer Knights Valley

Clos du Val

Geyser Peak Reserve

The Hess Collection, Cabernet, Sauvignon

Jordan

Joseph Phelps

Mondavi

Raymond

Ridge

Whitehall Lane

Chardonnay

Arrowood

Beringer Private Reserve

Chalone

Cuvaison

Ferrari-Carano

Kendall-Jackson Grand Reserve

Mondavi

Pine Ridge, Carneros

Sonoma-Cutrer

Merlot

Clos du Bois

Frei Brothers

Shafer

PINOT NOIR

Acacia

Au Bon Climat

Byron

Calera

Etude

Mondavi

Morgan

Saintsbury (Carneros)

SPARKLING

Chandon Reserve

Domaine Carneros

Iron Horse

Roederer Estate

SYRAH

Clos du Bois

Fess Parker

Justin

ZINFANDEL

Ridge Geyserville

Rosenblum-Continente

Seghesio Old Vine

OREGON

Argyle Pinot Noir

Willamette Valley Vineyards Pinot Noir

WASHINGTON STATE

Canoe Ridge Chardonnay

Chateau St. Michelle Chardonnay and Cabernet
Sauvignon

L'Ecole No. 41 Cabernet Sauvignon

Glossary

Acid: One of the four tastes of wine. It is sometimes described as sour, acidic, or tart and can be found on the sides of the tongue and mouth.

Aroma: The smell of the grapes in a wine.

AVA: Abbreviation for American Viticultural Area.

Bitter: One of the four tastes found at the back of the tongue and throat.

Botrytis cinerea (boh-TRY-tiss sin-eh-RAY-ah): A mold that forms on the grapes, known also as "noble rot."

Bouquet: The smell of the wine.

Brix (bricks): A scale that measures the sugar level of the unfermented grape juice (*must*).

Cabernet Franc (cah-burr-NAY frahnk): A red grape planted primarily in California and New York.

Cabernet Sauvignon (cah-burr-NAY so-vee-NYOH): The most important red grape grown in the world, yielding many of the great wines in the United States.

Chaptalization: The addition of sugar to the must (fresh grape juice) before fermentation.

Chardonnay (shahr-dun-NAY): The most important and expensive white grape, now grown all over the world; the best white grape of the United States, especially in California and Washington State.

Concord: A red grape used to make some American, primarily Eastern states' wines.

Decanting: The process of pouring wine from its bottle into a carafe to separate the sediment from the wine.

Estate-bottled: Wine that's made, produced, and bottled by the vineyard's owner.

Fermentation: The process by which grape juice is made into wine.

Jug wine: A simple drinking wine from California that is sold in "jug" bottles.

Long-vatted: A term for a wine fermented with the grape skins for a long period of time to acquire a rich red color.

Mechanical harvester: A machine used on flat vineyards. It shakes the vines to harvest the grapes.

Merlot (mehr-LOW): A red grape that produces great wines in California, Washington State, and Long Island.

Méthode Champenoise (may-TUD shahm-pen-WAHZ): The method by which Champagne is made.

Microclimate: A term that refers to an area that has a climate within a climate. While one area may be generally warm, it may contain a cooler *microclimate* or region.

Must: Grape juice before fermentation.

Nose: The term used to describe the bouquet and aroma of wine.

Petite Sirah: A red grape grown primarily in California.

Phylloxera (fill-LOCK-seh-rah): A root louse that kills grape vines.

Pinot Gris (PEE-noh GREE-ss): Also known as Pinot Grigio. Grown in California and Oregon.

Pinot Noir (PEE-noh nwahr): Very successful red grape of California and Oregon.

Reserve: A term sometimes found on American wine labels. Although it has no legal significance, it usually indicates a better quality wine.

Residual sugar: An indication of how dry or sweet a wine is.

Riesling: A white grape grown in the cooler climates of Washington State and New York.

Sauvignon Blanc (SOH-veen-yown blahnk): A white grape grown primarily in Washington State and California (where the wine is sometimes called Fumé Blanc).

Short-vatted: A term for a wine fermented with the grape skins for only a short time.

Sommelier (so-mel-YAY): The French term for cellar master, or wine steward.

Stainless-steel tank: A container that (because of its ability to control temperature) is used to ferment and age some wines.

Sulfur dioxide: A natural substance used in winemaking and grape growing as a preservative, an antioxidant, and also as a sterilizing agent.

Syrah (see-RAH): A red grape grown primarily in California.

Tannin: A natural compound and preservative that comes from the skins, stems, and pips of the grapes and also from the wood in which wine is aged.

Varietal wine: A wine that is labeled with the predominant grape used to produce the wine, i.e., a wine made from Chardonnay grapes (at least 75 percent) would be labeled "Chardonnay."

Viognier (Vee-own-YAY): A white grape grown primarily in California.

Vitis labrusca (VEE-tiss la-BREW-skah): A native grape species in America.

Vitis vinifera (VEE-tiss vih-NIFF-er-ah): The European grape species used to make both European and California wine.

Zinfandel (zin-fan-DELL): A red grape grown in California.

Index

Photo Credits

Smith & Wollensky Edition